POWERFUL LISTENING. POWERFUL INFLUENCE.

WORK BETTER. LIVE BETTER. LOVE BETTER.

BY MASTERING THE ART OF SKILLFUL LISTENING

TIM HAST

ISBN: 1490313559
ISBN-13: 9781490313559
Library of Congress Control Number: 2013910251
CreateSpace Independent Publishing Platform
North Charleston, South Carolina

For Ruthie,
Best friend. Best listener

TABLE OF CONTENTS

PREFACE

The old man and his wife spoke tenderly to each other the way young, excited lovers do upon discovering love for the very first time.

After spending most of a day with them, I asked how long they had been married—assuming they were widowers who had found each other in the autumn of their lives. He responded, "A long, long time." She grinned and said, "Sixty-two years." I then asked them, "What is your secret for such a long marriage?" Without missing a beat, he said, "We listen to each other."

An ancient Jewish parable tells a story about a man who was walking in a field and came upon a priceless treasure. The man in the story was honorable and did not take the treasure. Instead, he went home and sold everything he had in order to purchase the property where he found his fortune.

While the intent of the parable is not to illustrate the power of listening, there are points in the story that relate to this book.

First of all, skillful listening is a treasure that is worth whatever price it costs in order to possess it.

Second, it is hidden in plain sight for anyone to discover.

Third, it is worth the sacrifice you must make in order do it well. The parallels end here, because while listening is a treasure of great worth and hidden in plain sight, it costs absolutely nothing to possess, and anyone can, if he or she wants to become a good listener, accomplish just that with time and consistent practice.

My goal is for you to see the great value of this skill and begin the quest of owning what can't be bought, or sold, and is the foundation of lifelong success.

No matter what you do in life, becoming a good listener will only make you better: at work, at home, at loving others. It is the treasure—the secret to living well.

Chapter One

TORNADO!

"Listen closely to what I am saying.
That's one consolation you can give me."
Job 21:2

MAY 3, 1999

The sky was an eerie shade of green—a color that many who've survived a tornado in Oklahoma know very well. Late in the afternoon on May 3, 1999, people were headed home from work, having dinner, and going about their lives. The weatherman on the local TV affiliate said storms were coming and the chance of tornados was high. The "hook echo" in the storm cells, indicating the presence of a cyclonic formation, was clearly visible. But at that very moment, a group of tornadoes was already brewing that would cut a swath across the state.

According to the National Oceanic and Atmosphere Administration (NOAA), a system of seventy-four killer tornadoes hit over a three-hour span that afternoon, leaving $1.1 billion in damage in its wake. After the dust settled, ten thousand homes had been destroyed. Fewer than fifty people were killed, but thousands had their lives turned upside down.

The landscape was nightmarish. Heavy furniture was found sitting intact in prairie fields, miles away from the homes where it belonged. Photographs, important documents, and personal belongings littered the land. There were reports of semitrailer trucks and other massive equipment being hurled around like toys. Of all the incomprehensible sights, one particularly stands out in my mind. I remember seeing a large railroad boxcar sitting in a field a mile from the nearest tracks. No road, no other access—it had been hurled down from the sky. The way stuff was strewn all over the state came to be a metaphor for what had happened to so many Oklahoma families.

These were classified as EF5 category tornadoes, but, with wind speeds on the ground recorded at well over three hundred mph, their actual size and intensity went off the scale. The cyclones were some of the most powerful ever recorded. The news teams that took to the skies in the wake of the storms witnessed unimaginable scenes of destruction. From the sky it was easy to spot the two-hundred-yard wide trail of bare Oklahoma red dirt cut by the tornadoes. The cameras captured the vivid images of the muddy path the storms left as they cut across the land, leveling houses, demolishing property, and ripping the grass right out of the ground and the pavement from the roadbed.

But it was what couldn't be seen that turned out to have done the greatest damage.

•

AFTERMATH

Six months later, the community was rebuilding. Power lines were restored, houses were being rebuilt or repaired, and the infrastructure was returning to "normal." There was, however, a stark contrast between the reconstruction of houses and communities and their residents.

Many survivors were still hurting, nowhere near reconstructing their inner worlds. The communities affected by the storms were clearly suffering. Citizens were just beginning to experience marital discord, anxiety, insomnia, and difficulty concentrating. They reported they weren't doing well at work, and many were noticing unusual levels of anger and conflict at home. Children who were normally good students were unable to complete their assignments.

For these folks the wheels were falling off the car. Life was about as normal as a boxcar sitting in the middle of nowhere. The tornado was still ravaging their lives, keeping them in a constant state of total disarray.

I was part of a group of therapists hired through a Federal Emergency Management Administration (FEMA) grant to help these survivors cope with the fallout. Our team's assignment was to help the survivors sort through the pieces of the disaster and pull their lives back together. The federal government spent hundreds of thousands of dollars bringing in trauma experts to train local counselors on how to help clients deal with the issues related to their catastrophic experiences.

During this time, we received weekly training by the leaders in the field on the very best methods for treating disaster victims. The bulk of our job was listening to them tell their stories. Many of our interviews followed a pattern: *Where were you before the tornado hit? What warning did you have? What happened? What did you hear, feel, see? How did you survive? What happened afterward?* We interviewed and then counseled hundreds of survivors. The stories they told were often identical:

> *We were having dinner. The TV was on. The local weatherman cut into the programming to warn us about the tornado. We were advised to take precautions. This was a deadly tornado. Seek shelter. If you don't have a cellar, move to the center of your home and cover up with a mattress. We did. We heard it coming. Just like people tell you. It sounded like a freight train. It grew louder and louder. Then the house began to tremble and shake, then it disintegrated. Wind, dust,*

mud, insulation blowing, hitting us. Our faces stung. The sound was unbearable. Then silence, except for the sound of falling debris. After a few moments, we began to dig our way out, and then we smelled the gas. The tornado had sheared the homes off at the foundation and ruptured gas lines in house after house. The odor of natural gas was so strong that we went from fear of being blown away to fear of being blown up. Now, here it is six months later, and our family is always fighting. I'm not getting along with my coworkers. I can't concentrate. I can't sleep. What's wrong with me?

As we listened to their pain, we wondered, "How we could ever help these folks get their lives back to normal?"

They had the emergency funds from FEMA to rebuild their homes. There were plenty of community resources to help them replace their material goods and get on with their lives. But they needed something else a lot more. They needed to *talk* about their experience, and they needed to be *heard.* Our job was to listen to them and then help them find a way to heal and return to living.

As we worked with the survivors and attended to their stories, we began to see improvements in their lives. At first, all they could do was retell the same experience over and over, but from week to week, more details would surface. Their time with the therapist became the urgent priority in their lives. Often they would talk about how slowly the week went between sessions and how much they anticipated their next appointment. For a while they seemed to live from session to session.

This experience helped me see how important deep, intentional listening is in life. Research stresses how important it is for the victims of disasters to tell their stories in the presence of a "compassionate witness." The same thing is also true for the good health and prosperity of everyday people going about their normal lives.

The very skill that provides a lifeline for disaster victims is also essential to success to all areas of life, so we describe it as just that: *listening for success.*

WHAT IS LISTENING FOR SUCCESS?

Listening for success is deep, intentional listening and is called by various names: active, reflective, and empathic listening. It's simply seeking to understand the other person. It's the type of listening mental health professionals use in counseling, a way of attending in which the listener sets aside any agenda and attempts to be completely present in the moment with the speaker. The clear and powerful message is: "You are the most important person in the world to me right now, and I have all the time in the world to hear what you have to say."

Over my lifetime of working in the behavioral health field and in business, I have observed the most successful people I know share this common skill. They are *great listeners*, and *without saying anything at all,* they make you feel like what you have to say is the most important—in fact, the only—thing on their mind at that moment. Their words and body language communicate a clear message of openness, acceptance, focus, and safety. They have the ability to relate to and empathize with the speaker. They know how to put themselves in the other person's place, experiencing life from the speaker's perspective.

One of the things that set good listeners apart is that they instinctively put themselves in the speaker's shoes. My wife and I raised boys. When they were little and rascally, our friends who had only daughters would often look down on us as if we just didn't know how to make our children behave. That was, until those same friends adopted a little boy. Years later, after having walked in our shoes, they apologized for judging us. They had walked in our shoes and experienced and understood *our perspective.* This is what happens when people really listen. They walk in someone's shoes and experience his or her reality. They have that "aha" moment where they realize, "So that's what it feels like to be them; I understand now."

HOW DO WE TYPICALLY LISTEN?

The problem is most of us don't listen this way. We might read a good book on marriage, have this style of listening clearly spelled out to us, and attempt to focus on hearing our mate for a while. Or we might attend a workshop or seminar and leave with every intention of being a better listener. We acquire the knowledge but never really put it to use, so it's relegated to the back of the shelf and quickly forgotten.

When some famous psychologist on the morning show admonishes us to listen, we tell ourselves we probably ought to listen better. But how quickly our resolve dissipates like morning mist!

The problem is that we fail to see our own shortcomings. In surveys where people are asked to assess their own listening skills, most respondents are likely to say they believe they are good listeners. In fact, most people think they actually *are* adept at listening. However, the truth is that most of us really don't listen to others. Yes, we *hear* them, but we hear the facts, what we need to know, or what we want to hear. As a result, we miss the message that resides between the lines, which is often the real message begging to be heard. There is a lot more to listening than just hearing the sounds of another person's voice.

LISTENING BADLY: WHY DO WE LISTEN THIS WAY?

Being the eternal optimist, I believe there is something good in each of us, and most people generally have good motives behind their actions. There aren't many people who get up in the morning, look in the mirror, and say, "*I am going to be a bad listener today. I am going to do my best to ignore what people are saying to me. I am going to intentionally mistreat people.*" I'm convinced that most people don't think this way. We don't intentionally set out to ignore others; it just happens. I think for most of us, improving our listening skills is just very low on our priority list, or we don't fully understand what true listening requires or the benefits it provides. There are four reasons why we tend to be poor listeners, and at one time or another, we have all been guilty of one or more of these.

1. We're in a hurry.

The first reason we don't really listen is that we're in a hurry. I provide professional training in communication to large energy-producing companies in Oklahoma City. One of the hot topics I teach is time management. I show people how to use their time more efficiently and how to get the most out of the workday.

Many people waste time because they don't prioritize their tasks. By choosing the pressing issues over the important tasks, they never accomplish their top goals. So it is with listening.

We often fall into the penny-wise and pound-foolish thinking of assuming we don't have time to hear someone out. How often have you heard "I don't have the time to stand around all day and listen to him/her complain"? In our striving to get the job done, we want just the facts. We tell ourselves we don't have time for touchy-feely conversations; instead, we aim for maximum efficiency.

We have all kinds of gadgets that promise to streamline our lives and make better use of our time, but we must ask ourselves: Where is all that "saved" time going? It seems with all of our timesaving tools, we have done just the opposite. We don't have time for people, and thus we've created a monster, a black hole that sucks away all of our free time. We don't have time to sit and listen to a coworker, an employee, or a customer's needs. Because we are always in a hurry, we go from one meeting to another, to dinner, to get the kids to piano lessons, to the vet. Get here, go there. We are constantly on the run. This hectic pace doesn't allow for the intentional slowing down good listening requires. Who has time to stop and focus on what someone is saying? *"Just give me the facts, ma'am, and I'll be on my way. "*

So if I am to be a better listener, I must learn how to *slow down*. In order to improve your listening skills, you must figure out a way to stop and smell the roses or, better yet, pause and really hear someone's words. To do this requires a certain discipline and a commitment to catch yourself in the middle of your hurry and simply make yourself slow down, placing the other above yourself and focusing on the person who needs your undivided attention in that moment.

2. We're self-centered.

The second reason why we have such a hard time really listening to other folks is that we are self-centered. And we come by it honestly.

When you were a baby and you were wet, you cried. Chances are, someone picked you up and changed you. When you were hungry, you cried. Someone fed you. When you were sleepy... you get the point. You had a need, and you were sure to let people know you had a need, and that need was magically met. Somehow, they took care of you. This is a normal part of survival for babies, but sadly, long after we no longer need to use this strategy for survival, we remain stuck there, and we never shake the notion that the world revolves around us and our needs. As adults, this attitude plays out as, "I'm the center of the universe."

All of us tend to look out for "number one." After all, if you don't, who will? If you are a baby boomer, you were probably steeped in this way of thinking in the '60s. We are painfully aware of our needs, our feelings, our wants, and our desires. The problem is, we can be so driven to take care of our own needs that we become blind to the needs of others. Without making a conscious decision to focus on the needs of others, we might occasionally come up for air and, for a brief moment, become aware that there are others around us with their own sets of needs. But without intentionally being mindful of the needs of others, we are a lot more aware of what *we* want and what *we* need.

When we make the commitment to practice active, reflective, empathic listening, a very first step requires moving out of our world and our needs and stepping into another's reality. We must enter their world, their fears, their dreams, and *their* needs. Again, this requires premeditated, conscious action. I must choose to step into that person's world, and this requires that I divert the energy that goes into taking care of myself and use that energy to focus on someone else.

This is a skill that demands mindfulness and intentional actions to turn my attention to what someone is saying and focus on their words, as well as their world. This intentional focus on others is what we call "listening with your mind."

If I'm really honest, I must admit there are moments I don't want to move into someone's world. It's just too much trouble. I just want to go home, climb in my cave, and be left alone. At those times I realize just how much energy is required to move out of myself and into another person's story, and frankly—in that selfish moment—*I don't care.*

A simple principle brings this into sharp focus. If you want to be heard, you must earn that right by *first* listening to others—that is, of course, if you want other people to listen to you. Moving from being self-centered to being other-centered is the very attribute that gives us the opportunity to center the conversation back on ourselves. This is a great paradox. In listening, talking *less* earns you the right to be heard *more*, and people will in turn be more attentive to what you have to say. This all begins with moving out of self and toward others by cultivating an interest in those around you.

3. We don't know how.

The third reason why we don't listen the way we should is we simply don't know how to listen. It just isn't part of our educational curriculum. There is no course in any MBA program that I know of entitled "Listening 101." We don't teach people how to listen in elementary school, or in middle school, or in high school. Well-known mediator

Richard Salem writes:

> *(I) have come to understand, listening is a learnable skill. Unfortunately, it is not typically taught along with other communication skills at home or in school. I spend more time listening than using any other form of communication, yet as a youngster I was never taught the skill. I spent long hours learning to read and write and even had classroom training in public speaking, but I never had a lesson in listening or thought of listening as a learnable skill until I entered the world of mediation as an adult. While some may have had better experiences during their formative years, for many listening is often treated the same as "hearing." We do not ordinarily receive instruction in using our other senses—smell, sight, touch and taste—so why give lessons in hearing (sound)? A message that listening was an important skill to learn would have fallen on deaf ears when I was a child. Perhaps now that peer mediation is being taught in*

many classrooms across the nation, when children are taught to "listen to your elders," they also will be taught by elders who model good listening skills.

Listening is the principal tool that is used in psychotherapy. However, in my graduate training in counseling psychology, we only spent one semester where we were taught, among other topics, reflective listening. We spent a few weeks reading through scenarios and thinking up responses that would send "I hear you" messages to the client.

But for a profession that uses this tool 95 percent of the time, we had precious little practice with our most important skill. Yet I had a professor who frequently preached to our class, "If you listen to someone—really listen to them like they've never been listened to before—you will be far ahead of all your peers."

In education as well as business, there just isn't much in the way of training available to teach people how to listen.

I never forgot my instructor's admonition to listen. So, when I began working as a counselor and would find myself lost and confused in a client's story, wondering how to help him, I would return to the professor's mantra. The act of refocusing my listening on the client's story would get me, and the client, back on track.

As a therapist, I specialized in couples in high conflict. I discovered I was particularly effective in helping them mend their marriages. My success wasn't based on some exceptionally wonderful talent, some ancient secret wisdom, or brilliant psychological intervention. The one tool that enabled me to succeed in helping couples find happiness in their relationship was simple. I spent my time teaching them how to listen to each other, and so the therapy session became the classroom. Their assignment was to take the tools of skillful listening and apply them during the ensuing days. That is when the *real* therapy took place.

Couples who took this listening assignment seriously would often report back in the next session that they had experienced something new, a real breakthrough, and often they would begin with a comment such as one I heard from a CEO: "This stuff really works! We used it, and it helped our marriage! We used it on our kids, and it helped us! I used it at work with my employees, and it helped us!" It is amazing that just understanding *how* to listen and then doing it made all the difference in some relationships.

This particular experience allowed me to see how the very skills that helped couples in stormy relationships mend their marriages could be applied to relationship issues in the workplace, as well as any place where people must interact with each other. The key is knowing *how* to listen actively, reflectively, and empathically.

As I made the transition from therapist to executive coach, I found the same skills to be equally useful in coaching and facilitating and process work with groups, as well as in conflict resolution and mediation. These are skills that are not used like they should be for the simple reason that most people just don't know *how* to listen skillfully.

4. We shut it out.

The final reason why we don't listen is that we tune people out. Soon after we graduated from college, my wife and I found teaching jobs in a small town in rural Oklahoma. We found a wonderful "starter" house perfect in every way except for one thing: it was very near the railroad tracks. But the price was right, and we decided we could live with the noise.

At first, we noticed every time the trains passed, then a year later, we were oblivious to passing trains. We demonstrated what psychologists call *habituation*, which just means we became accustomed to that sound and tuned it out. This is natural, as we are engineered to shut out extraneous noise.

The brain has this amazing component called the Reticular Activating System (RAS), which, among other functions, is designed to filter out unwanted stimuli. At every waking moment, we are bombarded by so much sensory input that, if we attended to all of it, we would truly be driven to distraction. However, the RAS intercepts all of the random noise, or junk mail, that arrives in our brain, so we only attend to what it deems important.

The downside is that sometimes we begin to tune out the important stuff, such as what people are saying. We listen for pertinent facts (*what's in it for me*), and the rest becomes background noise, much like the sound that the teacher makes when she's speaking to the classroom in *A Charlie Brown Christmas*—"*Whah, whah, wa wa wa.*" And so we miss those important messages from others. We have tuned them out, because our brain is filtering out what it has mistaken for just more unnecessary noise.

RESEARCH SHOWS A DEEP-SEATED NEED TO BE HEARD.

What's amazing is learning to listen begins to take place even *before* birth.

French researcher Alfred A. Tomatis discovered we actually begin to listen even while we are still *in uteri*. As unborn babies, we are already learning to recognize our mother's voice. Tomatis found our ability to listen as adults is impacted by how well our prenatal listening abilities are developed. That bond is created before birth and is carried on into each developmental stage of childhood. When parents engage in deep listening with their infants, this exchange is thought to be an integral part of the development of a healthy brain.

A parent who hones in on his or her child's words and emotional messages is said to be engaging in a process called *attunement*. When the child coos or cries, the mother provides some feedback response that demonstrates that she is aware of her infant's needs. This responsiveness provides a sense of security for the child, and when a parent models this action, he or she lays the foundation for the child to become a skilled listener and, ultimately, underscores that good listening is critical to our well-being.

All this comes from listening deeply to a young child.

This investment of time and emotional energy provides the child a sense of security and confidence that accompanies them throughout his or her lifetime. If you meet children's emotional and attachment needs by listening to them, they will grow up with that model of attentive listening in their brains and, in turn, extend that same attentiveness to their own children and the other people in their world. Something in our biological make-up includes an intrinsic need to be heard and understood.

We all know complainers. You know, those whiny people who are always griping about everything and firmly believe their life's calling is to medicate the world with a miserable pill.

Think of some of these people in your life. Have you ever asked yourself *why* they are this way? Chances are, back in their early formative years, they had that need to be understood— the baby cried to get what she needed—and nobody addressed those needs. The chronic complaining is like a cry for help by a lost person calling out in the dark, "Is anyone out there?" They are like that baby, still trying to convince themselves someone really is there, listening, who understands their plight. So often their complaint is a problem so complex we recognize it is a hopeless case with no plausible solution in sight and, thus, we avoid them. They don't actually want someone to fix the problem. What they really want is just to be heard. There is a little frightened child inside, talking to whoever will listen, simply to make sure they are not alone in the dark.

SITUATIONS THAT CALL FOR POWERFUL LISTENING

Regardless of *why* we don't listen, the fact remains that failing to listen is a recipe for failure. Success in life requires us to slow down, become other-centered, and learn how to listen. Success in life also demands we *not* tune others out. If we are to be successful in relationships with our significant others, with our friends, and with our associates in business, we need to listen better. Moving beyond our own listening constraints and taking the time to focus on others is a powerful relational tool.

We can't afford the costly mistake of not listening.

There are those who call listening a soft skill and suggest that training on this topic is a waste of time and money. But that just isn't the case. Taking the time to listen well always pays off in the long run.

A 2002 Gallup survey revealed engaged employees—those who feel like management listens—could boost profits by 40 percent. Engagement is fostered where employees feel heard and understood.

A similar survey conducted by Sears determined a 4 percent increase in employee attitudes created a 4 percent increase in customer retention, which translated into $200 million in additional revenues over the following year. To me, there is nothing "soft" about two hundred million bucks of cold, hard cash. That's a pretty good return on investment.

The owner of a small business was summoned to an Equal Employment Opportunity Commission (EEOC) hearing. A former employee with an alternate lifestyle had filed a complaint against this company because two of the warehouse employees had made disparaging remarks about him. The owner of the business was expecting the worst-case scenario, such as a lawsuit and an astronomical fine that could cripple his business. So naturally, he was anxious about the possible outcomes, as well as bad publicity and morale issues among other employees.

But rather than coming to the hearing demanding financial reparations, the employee instead poured out his heart and expressed his disappointment that he wasn't protected from this sort of harassment. The owner chose not to get defensive and instead simply listened to him, empathized with him, and expressed his regret that he hadn't been aware of the situation. This was a powerful moment. In the end, the employee said he didn't want to file a lawsuit; he just needed to be heard. The EEOC levied a $1,000 fine—which is chump change compared to what it could have been—all because the owner took the time to really listen and attempted to understand.

Our success in life depends on this. My work now consists of teaching people the "soft skills" of business. Soft skills are communication, conflict resolution, teamwork, problem discussion, problem solution, customer service, and all the other interpersonal skills that provide the lubricant, enabling the engine of business to run smoothly.

I like to use the metaphor of a socket wrench set to describe this. If each of these skills represents a specific socket in a socket wrench set, then listening is the wrench handle. As important as it is to use a half-inch socket with a half-inch nut, without having the handle, having the right socket is still a useless proposition.

Listening is the handle that makes all the other communication and relational skills work.

You cannot build a great team if you can't listen. You cannot do strategic planning with your team, or even brainstorm. You can't sell, connect, or even relate to your loved ones. You will not lead your company without this skill. It is the hub of the wheel, and all the other skills are the spokes. It is the prime skill for success in business. Before you can master any other interpersonal skills, you *must* build a foundation on good listening skills.

WHAT'S IN IT FOR YOU?

In sales and training, it is important to present the need and the benefits that result when that need is addressed. A theory of adult education states that a person will learn when they know there is a benefit to making the effort to learn. Likewise, customers spend money when they perceive value in the product and the benefits it provides. The greatest benefit of becoming a skilled listener is that it simply makes life run smoother, both at work and at play.

At work, the most obvious benefit of being a great listener is career advancement. If you learn to listen well, you *will* advance in your career. A human resources manager told me of an energy exploration company seeking to hire a new vice president of operations. The company was not as concerned about finding someone experienced in the drilling industry as much as they were concerned that the candidate demonstrated good listening skills. Their assumption was it would be easier to teach a candidate the business of how to drill an oil well than it would be to teach a poor listener how to listen well.

An organization with good listeners stands to have a better chance at success. In addition to career advancement, when people really learn to listen, they handle conflict better and have healthy friendships with stronger bonds. Relationships run smoother when people are willing to really hear each other out. Learning to listen in the workplace just makes life generally go better.

Finally, if you need any more reasons to become a super listener, here is the best one of all: at home, listening is *great* for your love life. When we listen to our lover, we are making big deposits into the First National Bank of Love. When we fail to listen or say something inconsiderate or unkind, we make withdrawals. The goal is to make more deposits than withdrawals and avoid overdrafts whenever possible. Listening to your lover creates a deep bond of love and romance while keeping a positive balance in that account.

Even in conflict, skillful listening turns a bad situation around and can actually make a relationship stronger than before. Here's the scenario: a couple has had an ongoing argument. They really battle it out. They cry, they shout, they talk, and finally, in exhaustion, they get down to the real matter and speak from the heart. That deep connection is rekindled, and they make passionate love. What has actually happened is someone really listened and heard his or her lover's heart, which in turn, opened the door to deep intimacy. This is the big dividend for powerful listening. Every lover longs for a soul mate who can hear the deepest longing of his or her heart.

The bottom line is we just need to be heard. We have this deep longing that is satisfied when someone takes the time to listen to us with the goal of simply understanding us. To illustrate this point: I was at home early one afternoon working in the front yard when my wife returned from her monthly visit to the hair stylist. When she got out of the car, I could see she was visibly upset, so I asked her what was wrong. She said, "The most terrible thing has happened!" I imagined she must have witnessed a gory accident or some heinous crime. I asked again, "What happened?" She said, "Oh, it's just terrible," and then, after a wistful pause, she blurted out, "It's awful! My hairdresser is quitting the business!" As with every other guy in the galaxy, I'm biologically hardwired to "fix" things, and so naturally my response was, "Oh, honey, that's no big deal; we'll find you another hairdresser." When I tell this story at seminars, the guys always look at me as if to say, *Of course that's what you told her—what else would you say?* On the other hand, the women in the room look at me as if I had just said Hitler was my best friend. In that moment, she didn't need me to jump in and fix things. She just needed me to hear her, to understand just how upset she was, and to feel what she was feeling. Note for guys:

a woman's hairdresser is right up there in the same vicinity as God, Oprah, Mother Teresa, and Dr. Phil.

What I didn't get was she just *needed to be heard*. She needed me to hear her and respond from a deep level of empathy and understanding. She needed to hear; "Oh, I am so sorry. You must really be disappointed. Now you're going to have to go through the hassle of finding just the right one, who understands your hair and can do a good job." She just needed to be heard. No fix necessary. The whole world just needs to be heard, and blessed are those indeed who listen!

THE BOTTOM LINE

We all need to be heard. We humans have this particular need to be heard at a very deep level. This need is fueled by a question we all ask at some deep level: *Do I matter? Am I significant?* Much of what we do and say is an effort to assure ourselves we do indeed matter and truly are significant. Much of our longing to be heard is really a deep longing to be understood, to be known, and to be regarded as significant in the universe. We are so busy and so ignorant of this need, we try to outrun the distress that haunts us, and so we live harried lives. We make ourselves busy, perhaps in an attempt to cover up the void in our souls so we won't have time to stop and deal with the awareness that, deep inside, we are longing for something, and we don't even know what it is. This is what happens when our longings are undefined, vague, and beyond our grasp. We react by becoming frustrated, angry, and confused, and we medicate our distress with busyness.

Listening to others satisfies this longing by turning our focus away from ourselves and on those around us, and then we find fulfillment. Research is just beginning to confirm this experience as advanced imaging tools have enabled scientists to pinpoint places in the brain that become active when people engage in listening. Researchers have found that when two people are engaged in deep conversation, something powerful happens in the brain. Something brings people closer together and makes positive results happen, just by listening to another human being.

SUMMARY

When we were called upon to help in the aftermath of the tornadoes, our listening skills were the tools we used to help the victims. However, good listening skills are essential for successful living, both on a personal and a professional level. For most of us, becoming a good listener requires learning some new skills. If we can just slow down, get our focus off of ourselves, and become aware of others around us and the messages they are sending in their words and between the lines, we will become better listeners and better people, and we will enjoy increased success in our lives. Also, we will bless others in the process.

This book is about how to slow down and be aware of others around you. We will explore how to become a great listener. We discuss the different types of listening people use throughout their daily experiences—the three components of listening. We will discuss what not to do, and we will explore the poor habits that prevent good listening. We will introduce four simple skills to help you learn how to listen to others in a very powerful way. If you practice these skills and make becoming a great listener a lifetime quest, *you will be listening for success.*

ACTIVITIES: CONSIDER YOUR RECENT CONVERSATIONS

1. Think back over your conversations this week. What was the barrier that prevented you from being a better listener? In a hurry? Self-centeredness? Not knowing how? Or did you just unconsciously tune people out?

2. Which of the four barriers tend to interfere with your ability to listen?
    - ☐ In a hurry
    - ☐ Self-centered
    - ☐ Don't know how
    - ☐ Tune it out

3. In the coming week, be aware of your tendency to not listen and look for ways to overcome that particular barrier and improve your listening skills.

4. Picture that chronic complainer who you find yourself avoiding because life is so complicated and overwhelming to them. Next time you see him, remind yourself before you engage in conversation that you don't have to fix him. You are relieved of that duty. All you must do is just be present and listen.

Chapter Two

DO I *REALLY* HAVE TO LISTEN *?* (HOW IMPORTANT IS LISTENING?)

"The Universe is made of stories,
not of atoms. "
Muriel Rukeyser
Poet and social activist

I could see on my caller ID that it was my mother. I heard the pain in her voice from the very first moment I answered the call, and I knew she was clearly distraught. My parents are in those so-called golden years where they experience the frustrations of life from a senior citizen's point of view. Their health is declining, they are on a fixed income, and much of this high-tech world is confusing to them. So figuring out how to make ends meet can be very stressful. Her current upset: their water heater unexpectedly quit working. She had called a repairman who charged her a service call to come out and tell her she needed a new one, and then he tried to sell her a $4,000 water-heating system. Her sense of wariness was on high alert. To compound the issue, my father's poor health required her constant attention.

The demands of being a caretaker and not having hot water were clearly wearing on her. I tried to calm her down by reassuring her it would all get fixed. She began to tell me her frustrations, and I assured her that I understood just how she was feeling. With that comment, our conversation screeched to a halt, and I sensed her sudden distance over the telephone. She responded rather curtly, "There is no way you can understand what I'm going through right now."

My mother was absolutely right. With all my training, research, writing, and speaking on the topic of listening, I had failed from the get-go.

After recovering from her terse response, I paused, let go of my agenda, and assured her she was right. There *wasn't* any way I could possibly understand and, in fact, I didn't have any way to comprehend what it felt like to be her age and face the demands and frustrations that she was experiencing. The irony is that I'm supposed to know how this stuff works. I counsel, coach, lecture, and write on the topic; I'm "the expert," and, yet, I blew it. So I caught myself and started over, and I just listened to her as she recounted her troubles. As she spoke I could hear the anxiety leaving her voice.

In an instant I was reminded once again of how important simply listening is and the power it has to heal and encourage. All of us need good listening skills all the time. Now, more than ever, our ability to listen is closely linked to the degree of success we enjoy in this life, both on a personal and at a professional level.

In 1991, a study entitled "What Work Requires of School," by the US Department of Labor, described the level of preparedness for young people entering the job market and the specific skills needed to enable them to get good jobs and compete with their peers from other countries.

The underlying concern was, in a rapidly changing world marketplace, the United States needed to take a look at the preparation young people were receiving and assess the effectiveness of their training and readiness to enter the job market.

The researchers took a full year to interview business owners, employees, managers, union officials, line workers, and office workers. They canvassed retail, government, and manufacturing sectors.

The message they got was consistent from all quarters: for the youth of America to remain competitive with the world and get good jobs, *career jobs*, our schools needed to make serious, immediate changes. They concluded proper education required a new focus on specific skills to work smart in the coming years.

The study determined that for American children to be successful adults in the workplace, a new set of foundational skills and competencies needed to be taught in our educational system. The authors of this report went on to encourage parents to embrace the importance of these skills and competencies as well. They stressed the significance of teaching them both at school *and* at home as well as the need for a concerted and collaborative effort.

The researchers came up with five competencies that were built on three foundational areas of proficiency, the first three competencies were what we called in the old days "The Three Rs": reading, writing, and 'rithmetic (math). But in addition, the most intriguing recommendation was *listening*. They recommended listening skills be included in the curriculum.

While schools already teach the three basics, the absence of emphasis on listening is striking. The implication of the study is that listening expertise needs to be taught with the same intentionality and forethought as the other skills.

Here is the irony: we spend more of our day listening than anything else. Researchers Wolvin and Coakley observed most people spend about 9 percent of waking hours writing, 15 percent reading, 30 percent speaking, and 45 percent listening. Yet an emphasis on good listening lags far behind the other basic core proficiencies.

Interestingly enough, one must *first* be a good listener to be proficient at these basic competencies stressed by the Department of Labor study. Without listening skills, one might not ever learn math, reading, or writing. The other skills mentioned in the report depend on the ability to listen in order to master those skills as well.

How can you learn to solve math equations if your ability to listen, process, and respond is flawed?

Even in this study, the importance of listening is far understated, yet the implication comes through loud and clear. Good listening abilities provide the foundation on which the other success skills must be built.

The Department of Labor has found good listening skills rank high in order of priority, but we still haven't figured out how to include listening skills in our curriculum. It is ironic that twenty years after the report, there is no course on listening at the grade-school, mid-high, high-school, or undergraduate level, even with a preponderance of research to underscore the importance of listening. In contrast, research indicates the higher one climbs up the ladder of success, the more refined listening proficiency he or she will need.

In 1984, Watson and Barker discovered that executives spent anywhere from 55 to 75 percent of their time listening. The skill is just that essential to success, and yet there is not one course that I am aware of in an MBA program entitled "Listening 101."

IMPORTANT FOR PSYCHOLOGISTS (SHRINKS DO IT)

Powerful listening is central to psychotherapy. Research in the neuroscience of counseling psychology has found that physiological changes occur in the brain when a trauma victim recounts his or her experience to a compassionate listener. The victim often finds insight and meaning, and moves toward healing. This is the principal tool the clinician uses, as psychologists spend about 95 percent of their day listening. It's important because it works.

However, powerful listening is not the sole franchise of mental health practitioners. The rest of the working world has free access to this great tool.

One would suppose that because it is so essential to psychotherapy, graduate training would consist primarily of learning listening skills. However, in my graduate studies, I had two semesters of counseling classes, where one or two of the units actually included exercises in reflective or active listening. If the degree had been piano performance, the candidates would have been required to spend countless hours in a practice room. One would assume the same would be true for professional listeners. Skills require training, application, and continued practice, and powerful listening is a learned behavior that, like playing the piano, is improved with practice.

Yet there is precious little training or programs that provide mindful practice of the skill, even in areas of work and careers that depend on this ability.

IMPORTANT FOR SUCCESSFUL PEOPLE (WINNERS DO IT)

Beyond just getting *up* the ladder of success, powerful listening is essential to getting *along on* the ladder of success.

An employee is hired because he or she has the ability to do the job, but his or her ability to listen is what enables that employee to keep the job. It is the primary element in working through conflict, and it enables people to work through an adversarial standoff by moving conflicting parties from a win-lose to a win-win situation.

Powerful listening turns conflict from a destructive to a constructive force and to a means of achieving progress. It is the central component in conflict resolution and in mediation.

The most powerful reconciliation often happens when a mediator is able to bring two conflicting parties together and help them to truly hear each other.

Powerful listening enables adversaries in conflict to move beyond entrenched positions and deal with the real underlying issues. The shift that occurs with this movement often brings about resolution to conflict and results in successful mediation, which in turn reinforces the importance of listening. There will always be conflict at work and at home, but skillful listening is the catalyst that moves conflict from a destructive to a productive force.

When listening enables conflicting parties to work through their differences, often a stronger, more positive relationship emerges from the experience.

EVEN HUMAN RESOURCE PROFESSIONALS DO IT!

Good listening skills are essential to our individual success in the workplace, but they are also important for businesses as entities. An organizational culture that listens is a vital one, because listening provides a powerful resource for maintaining organizational health and success in the marketplace. One of the basic tenets of human resources is to hire good workers and take good care of them.

Listening is a big part of *retaining* good employees. When employees feel heard, they feel appreciated.

Another study released by the US Department of Labor concluded that 46 percent of those who quit their jobs did so because they felt *not listened to* and were therefore unappreciated. Consider this: *almost half the workforce* will leave their job because they didn't feel like their boss was listening. Moreover, ineffective listening throughout organizational structures has been proven to cause low morale, high absenteeism, low productivity, lack of upward communication, and ineffective horizontal communication.

The research then and now points to the same conclusion: individuals who don't feel "listened to" don't stay in that job very long. High turnover carries a hefty price tag and has a significant impact on the health and well-being of an organization, as well as the bottom line.

IMPORTANT FOR MANAGEMENT

The ability of management to listen to their employees has a definite impact on the company's level of productivity. If management fails to listen, businesses fail to thrive. Individuals, teams, and entire organizations suffer when leaders neglect to listen to employees and customers. This is clearly illustrated in the story of two large retail stores.

IMPORTANT FOR INDIVIDUALS: BEST BUY VS. CIRCUIT CITY

Robert Tucker, president of The Innovation Resource Consulting Group, describes a tale of two companies. He noted that when facing troubled times, Circuit City fired their experienced salespeople and hired lower-wage replacements in the interests of cutting costs, but the strategy didn't save the company. Tucker goes on to compare this with another electronics retailer company. He notes that when times were tough, Best Buy focused on creating a deeper dialogue with their 160,000 employees.

Simply put, they started listening. They conducted weekly online polls of employees. They provided internet chat rooms called Wikis where employees with common interests could connect to discuss issues. They established weekly town-hall meetings for managers, and they came up with the "listening chair," a format where employees could survey each other on all types of issues concerning sales and merchandise. When they launched this revolution, their employee turnover rate was sitting at 81 percent annually. Three years after implementing this new culture of listening, that rate dropped to 60 percent. A year later, it had dropped to 40 percent.

Here are two companies that went in opposite directions. One fired its talent and failed; the other listened to its talent and succeeded.

It would be nice to say that this change in culture came about because the folks at the top had an epiphany and started listening. That just wasn't the case.

Instead, Jennifer Rock, a midlevel marketing manager, discovered how *not* communicating was costing the company dearly. She stepped up to the plate and did something about it by creating her own position: Director of Intranet and Dialogue. She had a clear vision of what she needed to do, which was "whatever it takes to help Best Buy become extraordinary at communicating with employees and to connect employees with information and with each other as well."

She got the point. She understood this simple principle: if you listen to your employees and help them succeed, you *will* help the business succeed. She accomplished this by intentionally creating a climate and culture of listening. She understood the importance of listening.

Everyone who has been in business knows of someone who failed to listen and the dire consequences they faced as a result of their failure. The workplace, the morale, and a company's performance all improve when management recognizes this skill deficiency as a cultural norm and takes a decisive course of action to change the behavior.

IMPORTANT AT THE TOP

As we previously noted, most people spend about 45 percent of their waking hours listening. But the higher your position in life, the more you must listen to be successful. This percentage of time spent listening increases proportionately as you advance upward. At the very top level of management, executives will spend 60 to 75 percent of their time listening. In the rarefied air of the corporate suite, careers live or die by how competent executives are with this ability.

A.G. Lafley became the CEO of Procter and Gamble in 2000. When he joined the company, it was a traditional top-down, do-what-I say, silo-prone culture. After eight years under his leadership, that same company had become far more collaborative and innovative and, as a result, *company revenues doubled.*

Friends characterize Lafley as a modest, soft-spoken man who had nerves of steel when it comes to tolerating risks. He was also known for his incredible ability as a strategist. While those factors certainly contributed to his success, something that might not be quite so apparent has been his ability to communicate, the primary component of which is listening well. He has a reputation for being an expert in this realm.

As the CEO, he was careful to remind his team again and again of this simple mantra: "The consumer is boss." He wanted those around him to know, ultimately, it is the person who buys the product whose opinion needs to be heard.

In keeping with what he preached, he left the building. He went out to the consumer and listened. He left his office and traveled the nation and the world. His goal was to meet with "the boss"—the consumer—on his or her own turf. He met them in their homes and out shopping. His goal was to cut out the middleman and find out directly from his customers what they bought and why. He didn't stop with the consumer. He took the time to speak and listen intently to his colleagues. He had discovered one of the great secrets of leadership: you don't take the helm and succeed because you know so much. You succeed because you *listen* so much. He understood the importance of listening, and he understood good leadership *is* good listening.

THOSE THAT DON'T DO IT DON'T LAST.

Contrast Lafley with the myriad of has-been CEOs who throughout their careers chalked up some impressive victories but, because of their inability to communicate, or more specifically, listen to those around them, ended badly. You can have great instincts, strategies, and leadership qualities but without good listening skills, your abilities are seriously flawed. When leaders communicate badly, they make it much more difficult to communicate what they expect from their subordinates. These expectations must be clearly stated from the very first moment on the job.

The transfer of information and communication of expectations require hearing as well as speaking. When expectations are vague, the potential for conflict abounds, because misunderstanding breeds conflict. Where misunderstanding is present, conflict will inevitably happen.

Lack of clear expectations is the spawning ground for discontent and disengagement, and clear communication and listening need to start with a new employee's first day on the job. The only way one can ensure that what he or she is saying is actually understood is to solicit feedback. In order to do this, one must listen to that feedback to ascertain that what was heard actually matches up with what was said.

Much research has gone into the science of onboarding—a term that describes the time spent opening a new position, recruiting, interviewing, hiring, training, and assimilating a new hire into the organization. Studies indicate a new employee works under a cloud of uncertainty and anxiety when he or she does not have a clear sense of what is expected of them.

A manager who is skilled at listening will pick up on this anxiety before it becomes a problem. When bosses don't listen, they don't have good data on which to base their decisions and actions or understand the needs and concerns of the new team member. Without the proper information to make good decisions, the team member eventually fails.

Unfortunately, powerful listening is not necessarily a trait we are born with. It is a multifaceted behavioral skill that must be learned, practiced, and improved over time. Then, the manager must consistently model these behaviors for it to become part of the company culture.

Business journalist John Huey notes most CEOs have about eighteen months to prove themselves at the top. Huey observes that if they haven't gotten the job done by then, they will probably be out looking for a new position. The pivotal skill that makes the difference between success and failure for many is how well they listen to those around them. He states top executives are on a collision course with trouble when they quit listening to the shareholders and stakeholders.

For many, it is not that they quit listening to everyone. Rather, they become *selective*, surrounding themselves with a few trusted advisors. As a result, these executives often receive poor or skewed information, because they aren't balancing that selective source with a cross section of input from employees and customers.

The bottom line is they become selective listeners by limiting the people they are listening to, resulting in a distorted picture of reality.

They become isolated from the voices that matter the most, and this betrays their ignorance as to the importance of listening.

They are refusing to look at the big picture or the entire picture. Their information is skewed and, thus, their decisions are flawed.

The day they make it to the top is often the very last day they will ever hear the truth, especially if they quit listening to all but a few in the inner circle.

IMPORTANT FOR CEOS—GOOD FOR BUSINESSES

During the 2008 recession, the automotive industry took a beating. While GM and Chrysler were in bankruptcy—and much of the industry was propped up by government loans—Ford Motor Company earned $2.6 billion in sales in its second quarter of 2010. This stands in stark contrast to Ford's $424 million loss the previous year. So how did they manage it?

The facts point to the arrival of CEO Alan Mulaly, who was hired by Ford after having worked for thirty-seven years in the aviation industry. There was skepticism in Detroit because he wasn't a "car guy."

But that didn't deter Mulaly.

He jumped in the driver's seat, took the wheel, and put the brakes on the number of models offered by Ford. He universalized them so that a Ford is a Ford, no matter where in the world you buy it. The Ford Focus you purchase in Buenos Aires will be the same exact car you might purchase in Quebec.

Until Mulaly, there were regional variations in the same car worldwide. When purchasing parts for a certain model, you had to make sure you stipulated where that particular Ford was manufactured, because not all parts were created equal or were compatible.

That is no longer the case since the advent of the new leadership. This cost-saving move was called, aptly enough, "One Ford," an innovation that came from bringing all the parties and departments to the table by knocking down the walls of silo thinking, exposing departmental secrets, and leading the pack in listening to each other.

Mulaly demanded that all departments provide complete disclosure and required that each department and division be heard. He instituted a meeting every Thursday of two hours and fifteen minutes where teams in this new paradigm would share all performance data. Previously, there was information-hoarding that was costing Ford big bucks.

But Mulaly led the company toward a culture of open communication and ostensibly of *truly* listening to each other for the first time. The success of the company in such troubled times speaks for itself.

Incidentally, just the move from local fiefdoms to the "One Ford" concept raised their profitability by 20 percent. All of this is because a CEO valued what Ford employees had to say, decided to remove the barriers that prevented management from listening to each other, and created a listening culture in the company.

The point that you will observe again and again is that listening is critical for the bottom line.

THE MCDONALD'S STORY

In the final quarter of 2002, McDonald's reported its first quarterly downturn since becoming a public company back in 1965. This was a super-size loss of $343.8 million. A gloomy article published that year eulogized the company and mourned the tarnishing of McDonald's golden arches. The downturn of McDonald's was a combination of a "bigger is better" and a "let's just build more stores and up-sell more" philosophy. The fast-food behemoth was facing nutritionally-based lawsuits, changing customer tastes, and worldwide protests. They had become the hamburger store everyone loved to hate.

The story, however, does not end there.

Company leaders began to take stock of their predicament and developed a strategy that is simple yet incredibly profound. They returned to basics and became intensely customer-focused, coming up with a simple but elegant plan.

They realized that if they were to be successful, they had to do three things: listen, learn, and lead.

First: *listen to the customer.* "Doing the right thing is at the core of McDonald's values. This recognition reflects our accountability to our customers and our strong commitment to listening, learning, and leading the way in key industry changes," stated Bob Langert, vice president of corporate social responsibility. They were reminded "the customer is the boss," so learn from the customer and, finally, lead from what you have learned. What a novel idea! They *did* listen and, from that they learned, they led.

It turned the company around. They would have spared themselves *and* their stockholders a lot of misery if they had only realized the importance of listening at the beginning.

ASK THE QUESTION AND LISTEN!

Research stresses the importance of listening for an organization. Ask the question and listen, and you *will* get the information you need to succeed. That is, if you are courageous enough to listen to the unvarnished truth.

Often, we listen to good news but turn a deaf ear on the bad. Then, if we listen at all, we tend to listen in order to explain ourselves, or we listen and remain undeterred in our goals. For companies that recognize they don't listen but want to change, there is a simple solution: start doing research. Ask your customers questions, start listening, and brace yourself for the answers being willing to hear them out without excuses, deflection, or defensiveness.

I recently read a blog posting by a well-known business consultant who disparaged the act of listening to customers. He wrote that you will constantly be changing unnecessarily and eventually run yourself out of business by responding to every little complaint and making changes every time a customer has a problem. He had an "amen chorus" of people who wrote replies agreeing with his blog.

However, I believe he missed the point. Listening is not the problem. Instead, the real problem is the knee-jerk reaction to every complaining customer. His confusion comes from not understanding the difference between a *position* and an *issue*. A position is the event on the surface and an issue is the deeper-rooted problem.

Skillful listening is required to discriminate between positions and issues.

You will be running yourself ragged and not getting anywhere if you are constantly reacting to the positions people take. However, if you are truly listening to your customers, you will soon move beyond hearing *positions*, which are the complaints on the surface. Instead, you will uncover the real *issues* or the deeper, hidden problems. Paying attention to these make the organization stronger, healthier, and much more effective.

Powerful listening moves you from reacting at a superficial level to hearing what your customers really want and expect from you. It helps you understand the deeper message written between the lines. It helps you get down to the real issue and not just the chatter and complaints that the blogger was writing about.

A word of warning, however: be prepared to listen to the truth, no matter how painful, show your customers you are listening, and then thank them sincerely for their help. A customer's complaint is a gift and a favor. It is the cheapest research money can buy, and it reveals something specific that needs to be addressed in order to make the organization better. For the complaining customers, just listening to them is powerful. Often, complaining customers just need to be heard, and this alone is, for many, the "fix."

If your shipment arrived late, you can't rewind time and do it over. The best you can do is empathize, apologize, understand, and ask for a chance to make it up to the customer. Chances are you'll make better customers out of them. McDonald's has proven this by becoming the poster child for the cause of skillful listening in an organization.

LISTEN TO COMPLAINTS

The research firm TARP has found that for every upset customer who complains, twenty-six others don't. So, if ten customers have complained recently to your company, another 260 may have held their tongues while turning to your competitors. *Really listening* to complaints is your best research tool and provides a way to get to those issues employees and customers bring up. It's also the cheapest way to get the feedback you need to improve your business.

Don't be afraid of complaints; instead, be thankful for them!

A customer who expresses a complaint to you is a valuable asset. The one who doesn't complain to you, or goes unheard, destroys your business. In the age of Facebook, complaints move through cyberspace at breathtaking speed and efficiency. With the advent of social media, everyone is empowered with a voice and a soapbox in the town square. If you mistreat your customers, or ignore their complaints, they have the power to "tweet" you right out of business. When you listen and respond, you are doing what you need to do to make your business better.

IF IT'S GOOD FOR THE GOOSE

The experience that fueled my fervor about the importance of powerful listening started years ago as a therapist working with couples in troubled relationships. Many had seen a string of therapists before me, and most seemed pretty hopeless about their future together.

I had been trained in a listening and communication model that was developed by researchers at the University of Denver, which is based on the work of John Gottman, Cliff Notarius, and other pioneer researchers in relationship issues.

I observed the couples who succeeded at improving their marriages were the ones who learned and faithfully implemented the communication strategies discussed during their therapy session. There were many times while coaching a couple through a difficult topic, the listener would say with compassion and empathy, "You never told me that before." Often the reply would be, "I did, but you just never listened until now."

The breakthroughs for these couples often occurred when they set aside their own agenda and defenses and really heard each other for the very first time.

I remember one couple I helped right after I finished my graduate training. Their relationship was severely "at risk." They constantly fought, and the conflict would often escalate into physical violence. One or the other would frequently pack up and leave. As a young, inexperienced therapist, I entertained very little hope for them. But I used the only technique I knew: listen to them and help them listen to each other.

Fast-forward many years later. I was in a new career as a professional trainer and performance coach. I was facilitating a training session, and recognized the wife as one of the participants. Even though I tried not to make a big deal of it, she pointed at me and announced to the entire class: "He used to be my therapist. My husband and I fought all the time. That was a long time ago, and we were talking about that the other day because we realized we hardly ever fight anymore."

The healed marriage wasn't because of my skills. It wasn't magic. It was the power of listening. They enjoyed success in their relationship because they discovered the importance of listening to each other.

Listening is important for individuals, management, CEOs, organizations, and people in general, and in any relationship.

IF LISTENING IS SO IMPORTANT...

So, now you realize the importance of listening. Consider this: Who is your favorite friend? *The one who listens!* From all fronts, the message is consistent. Listening is an important ingredient of success in business and in life.

So why don't we see more of an emphasis on mastering listening skills in our educational curricula? Why don't we see a curriculum that purposefully focuses on cultivating this skill beginning in kindergarten and continuing on through graduation? The answer is, for many people, it just seems too simple a concept to be of real concern. Perhaps the belief is *nothing that simple could actually work that well.* I have to wonder how it might impact our workforce, the divorce rate, and the dockets of civil cases in our court systems if such a course of study were a reality in our schools.

Powerful listening works powerfully in every area of life where two or more people have to work together. It is essential for healthy relationships, whether at work or at home.

My phone conversation with my mother mentioned earlier was sobering on more than one level. It's difficult to see your parents struggle and not be able to step in and do something to shield them from this passage in their lives. Because they're our parents, it's also difficult to just listen to them and hear their pain. After all, they are the parents, *my* parents. They are supposed to be the ones who listen to us, and now the role has been reversed.

After our conversation, my mother still had to deal with getting her hot water problem resolved. My dad's health issues didn't go away. Our chat didn't restore the lost years of life or turn their retirement into bliss.

But having been listened to and understood, my mom was able to make it through the day with a sense of hope that she didn't have before—all because she was heard, and that alone made the difference. For my mother, being listened to—just being heard—*was* important enough.

ACTIVITIES : HOW IMPORTANT IS IT TO YOU?

1. Monitor the amount of time you spend listening for a week.

   Just how much of a priority do you place on listening? Make an inventory of the percentage of your own time you spend listening to others. Take a sheet of letter-size paper, turn it horizontally (landscape vs. portrait), and at the top, draw seven columns—one for each day of the week. On the left side, make sixteen lines for the hours of the day that most of us are awake, say from 6:00 a.m. to 10:00 p.m. Now find a quiet place to sit and clear your mind and think back over the past seven days. Begin to notice when in that schedule you listened to others. After you have completed this inventory, please notice how much of your time was spent listening.

2. How often do you find yourself trying to "fix" someone when they come to you with a problem? Imagine what it would be like if you didn't feel this responsibility when people speak to you. Give yourself permission to listen just to understand the other person, and set yourself free from the responsibility to fix everyone.

3. For one week, try to listen all the time and not speak unless you absolutely need to. Notice what you feel as you try this activity.

41

Chapter Three

SO, *ARE* YOU LISTENING? MASTERING THE ART OF LISTENING FOR SUCCESS

"Hear this, you…
who have eyes but do not see,
who have ears but do not hear…"
Jeremiah 5:21

Jill was angry. The report she asked Brian to finish a week ago appeared on her desk yesterday, just hours before the big meeting. Jill needed that information and was counting on Brian to do an exhaustive, detailed report. What he had in his hands appeared to be a summary, an outline of the information.

Jill went to Brian's office. Brian was working on his computer as Jill knocked on the door. Brian welcomed her but continued working on his keyboard.

"We need to talk about this," Jill said as she dropped the report on Brian's desk. "I asked you to do a thorough analysis, and you gave me a Wikipedia article. This is unacceptable. It's garbage!"

Brian blushed, shoved his keyboard tray back on his desk, and glared at Jill.

"You didn't say it needed to be that detailed. You said you just needed bullet points."

"I said I needed an analysis, and you could summarize it at the beginning in bullet points, but I expect you to get off your butt and do some work around here."

Brian smacked his hand down on the desk and said, "You need to be clearer about what you want. You're always giving me work to do without telling me exactly what you need, and I'm tired of having to read your mind."

This is a conversation that is headed downhill, picking up speed, and most likely won't end well. If someone could intervene at this point and require Jill and Brian to engage in skillful listening to each other, that bad ending might be averted. In order to change the ending, one must understand the mechanics of skillful listening and the hazards that crop up along the way.

HEARING VS. LISTENING

By now you're probably wondering, what *is* listening for success? How is it any different than any other listening, and why particularly do I need to read a book on listening?

In an episode of the TV show *Everybody Loves Raymond*, the main character, Raymond, and his wife were having a disagreement about whether or not they should attend a parenting class. In the middle of the discussion, he blurts out, "Why do we need to take a class on parenting? That's like taking a class on smelling."

You might ask a similar question: "Why read a book on listening? Doesn't everybody know how to listen?"

There is more to listening than just hearing. We hear even when we're asleep, but we often fail to listen when we're fully awake. There's an old saying, "Most people tend to be hard of listening rather than hard of hearing." Listening requires focusing on what we're hearing.

THE ANATOMY OF SKILLFUL LISTENING

In order to move beyond just hearing, you must understand and master the three components of skillful listening: *sensing, processing,* and *responding.* When you actively engage in all three, you are really listening. When you leave one of these components out, you are just hearing and most likely missing the point of the message.

THE CAMERA METAPHOR

The best way to illustrate the mechanics of skillful listening is to use a digital camera as an illustration. It has three basic components: the lens, which gathers and focuses the light; the semiconductor image panel, which absorbs the light and turns it into an image; and the LCD screen on the back of the camera, which enables you to view the image the camera has captured.

SENSING

Sensing is the first step in listening. Using our camera metaphor, it is the equivalent of the lens. There is an entire spectrum of information we are gathering when sensing, whether we are at one end of the continuum listening for facts, or at the other end, listening for emotions and connection. Either way, we are sensing. We're focused on gathering data.

I really caught the gotta-have-it fever when digital cameras first hit the market. But I hesitated to buy one until I could afford a model with great definition. I finally found just the right one made by a company that has a long history of manufacturing quality products. The camera took nice pictures. However, I was always a little dissatisfied with their lack of sharpness. A few years after learning to live with this frustration, a professional photographer told me the problem is not the camera but in the stock lens that comes with it. He said I would get the quality of sharpness that was eluding me if I were to invest in a professional grade version of the lens that particular company made for their cameras, which incidentally, cost twice what I paid for the camera itself. In order to take professional-quality pictures, I needed a lens that could accurately *sense* the details that I was trying to capture in my pictures.

In the same way, great listeners try to get the whole picture.

So how do we improve our listening perception? How do we upgrade our lens, or sensing abilities? By becoming aware of what impairs accurate sensing and learning how to compensate for those impairments.

In using the camera metaphor, our perception is sometimes hindered by a dirty or defective lens, or improper lighting. Sensing is the lens where the input is gathered.

In the parallel for listening, this is the process of perceiving the essence of the speaker's message. Good sensing requires that we get as much information as possible without distorting that information—i.e., using bad optics, a scratched, tinted, or dirty lens.

We distort or filter what we perceive when we have preconceived notions, or arrive at premature conclusions about what we are hearing. In the opening vignette, Jill was already angry and convinced Brian wasn't pulling his own weight. Her anger became a filter that prevented Jill from getting the full story.

Perhaps you've had a conversation where you thought the person was saying one thing when they were actually talking about something completely different. We might have filters that keep us from getting some of the information, or we might have already had another picture in our head just before the conversation started. They took the conversation in one direction, and we went in another.

We are sensing the messages between the lines when we are listening comprehensively. We are sensing what the other person is experiencing or feeling if we are engaging in empathic listening. Or, on the other extreme, we might completely miss the emotional content of the message if we are listening for facts. We are sometimes so focused on one part of the message that we miss the other parts.

In our opening story, Jill was missing a lot because she was sure she already had the answer.

UNDERSTANDING FILTERS THAT DISTORT SENSING

Conditions prevent us from hearing or cause us to filter out part of what we're hearing. You need to understand filters, because they come between us and the speaker and prevent the listener from getting the entire message. Filters can be external, internal, topical, or gender- or generational-based, and can also be related to our particular personality style.

External filters are background noise: the environment, the pretty, shiny objects that distract us. In order to really listen, you need to be able to control the external distractions. Some places are just not conducive to good listening. If you're trying to have a deep conversation in a crowded, noisy restaurant, you probably won't listen (or hear) very well. In sports bar restaurants, the walls are lined with TV screens showing every imaginable sport, constantly streaming the latest images. These are difficult places for me to focus on the speaker.

External filters can be the room temperature, the noise level, the number of people and their proximity. All of these things can distract us from truly listening.

When I meet someone for coffee, I always try to sit facing an area where I won't be distracted by a TV or other people passing by. I understand my own tendency to be distracted and how it can filter out my ability to listen, so I try my best to compensate for my distractibility.

Internal filters have to do with who we are and what is going on in our inner world at any particular moment. Who we are includes our gender, personality style, occupation, and even our particular generation. Try as we might, it is impossible for us to hear every nuance of what others are saying. Each of us tends to filter out some of the message and focus on other parts.

Think of this as a spectrum where at one end a listener is filtering out everything but the facts, and at the opposite end another listener is filtering out everything but the emotions.

There are at least five specific ways that the listener filters the content of the message: **critical**, **discriminative**, **comprehensive**, **appreciative**, and **empathic** filters. Each of these types of listening is focused on achieving a specific task to be accomplished by listening and represents a specific piece of the pie.

The problem is that when listening is focused on a specific goal, other important issues tend to get filtered out of the message. In a perfect world, the listener would sense all the varied and subtle nuances. Unfortunately, the world isn't perfect and neither are we. It is difficult for anyone to tune in to all five areas without some filtering.

CRITICAL LISTENING FILTER

Critical listening is focusing on the words and the facts those words convey for the purpose of understanding, evaluating, and then assigning meaning to what the listener has heard, while filtering out everything else. The critical listener seeks to gather *factual* information. An engineer asks another engineer about the strength of a certain mix of concrete. He doesn't want to know what the other engineer *feels* about concrete. He wants facts, numbers, and statistical evidence to inform his decision.

I was hired to help a C-level executive who was struggling with what the human resources person described as some "interpersonal problems," but I wasn't told exactly what the problem was. It seemed that this executive was well liked but those who directly reported to her didn't enjoy interacting with this person, but they couldn't put their finger on *why*.

The problem became very clear in our initial session. This executive talked about not having the time for chit-chat, or the patience for listening to explanations of why a certain action was taken. This person wanted the facts—the results—with a minimum of discussion.

Coworkers and direct reports were put off by what they perceived as this manager's abruptness and impatience: "I don't have time for all of that. I don't need to know how they feel about it. I just need to know that they did it, and whether or not it was effective." For this individual, anything more than that was just a waste of time.

This critical listening approach had a negative effect on the team, and its productivity level plummeted. Sadly, this manager's listening skills were limited to critical listening, and this imbalance in skills hindered her effectiveness. She was out of a job within a year.

CEOs who struggle with interpersonal relationships and problems with teams probably do so because they are solely focused on this aspect of listening. Their listening is strong on specific areas of perception but weak on processing and responding. It is imbalanced. It is like having a car with an accelerator but no brakes.

DISCRIMINATIVE LISTENING FILTER

Discriminative listeners seek to "listen between the lines" or listen for facts or meaning that is implied by means other than the words. Discriminative listeners will watch the body language for meaning. They will listen to the inflection of the words as well as the message in the words and decide whether or not both are congruent.

Discriminative listeners analyze all perceived input to determine if it is conveying something other than what it appears to be. For them, words, inflection, and body language must line up and, when they don't, the discriminative listener will discount the message. The discriminative listener is focused on consistency.

Our words, inflections, and body language must match for us to be credible. For example, you can say "I love you," and your tone, inflection, and body language can confirm that you really mean what you say. Or, you can say "I love you"— the exact same words—but you lace those words with sarcasm, a cold inflection, and contradictory body language. That same phrase will take on a whole new meaning. The discriminative listener will pick up on the words saying "I love you" as well as the actual unspoken, but ever-so-clear message: "I'd like to run over you with my pickup truck."

Discriminative listening distinguishes differences between the words and the unspoken message and determines if the two are consistent or contradictory.

Law enforcement officers, human resource professionals, and journalists rely on this type of filter. An attorney or investigator might examine a witness and look for body language or voice inflections that could reveal or betray the veracity of that person's testimony. If you are interviewing someone for a position, posture tells you a lot about the interviewee's confidence level. Their words might say "I want this job," but their inflections might betray a complete lack of confidence in their own abilities to actually do the work required. Without accurate perception, the information gathered is flawed and without accurate processing, discriminative listening is also flawed because those who have this filter tend to be skeptical about the veracity of message.

As you can see, there are situations where you must attend to one particular part of sensing and consequently filter out the other information.

COMPREHENSIVE LISTENING FILTER

When you engage in comprehensive listening, the third type of filter, you are intensely focused on the message with the sole purpose of simply *understanding the person.*

When people listen comprehensively, they intentionally withhold any type of critical judgment or conclusion about the message. For example: imagine you have a dear friend whom you love to be around. Her only flaw is that she is on the opposite side of the political spectrum from you. Also imagine you are having a conversation about her political beliefs, because you really want to know *why* she embraces those particular views. You're not asking so you can draw her into an argument or make a judgment; you just want to see things from *her* perspective. Therefore, you withhold judgment and you just listen, because you want to understand *why* she sees the world the way she does. You want to comprehend her point of view.

When we don't have all the facts or know *why* a person is taking a specific action, we tend to interpret those actions in the worst possible light. Yet when we behave in a specific way, we expect people to always give us the benefit of the doubt or interpret our actions as motivated by altruistic motives.

Comprehensive listening seeks to override this tendency to regard the motives of others with a skeptic's eye and instead, it seeks to *comprehend,* to give others the benefit of the doubt until you know, factually, why they are behaving in a certain way.

This is truly a way of extending grace to others. The benefit of this particular filter is that it draws the speaker to the listener and creates connection. The problem is that sometimes important information is overlooked in giving others the benefit of the doubt.

The comprehensive listening filter suspends judgment and the search for facts and veracity and focuses on simply hearing the speaker's point of view. Again, while we strive to broaden our perception, there are times when focusing on one particular aspect of the message and filtering out the rest is beneficial.

APPRECIATIVE LISTENING FILTER

The fourth type of listening filter is appreciative listening, the process of listening for enjoyment.

For example, I am listening for enjoyment when I listen to my grandson tell about his favorite video game or the giant fish he caught. I am engaged in appreciative listening if I am listening to someone tell a story or relate an experience with no purpose except to be captivated by the story.

Appreciative listening affects your life the most when you make the point to see something good in everyone. This technique has a tremendous impact on those around you, and the appreciative listener looks for opportunities to do this.

Appreciative listening is done for sheer pleasure; it conveys trust and anticipates good things. It expects the best of others, and it gives them the benefit of the doubt. It is optimistic and anticipatory, and it assumes people have a great story to tell, something interesting to say. This type of listening always believes in people and their best motives, that they are telling the truth until proven otherwise.

Appreciative listeners approach others with the attitude, "There's a good story here if I take the time to listen." The world could use more appreciative listening. The really famous people I have met who made a positive impression on me are people who, when introduced, treated me like I was someone very important and fascinating. By listening appreciatively to someone, you are conferring great value on him or her. The act of being present and engaged, combined with delight in hearing someone's story, communicates "you are important!" I *do* feel important when someone I perceive to be powerful and influential focuses on me this way.

The problem is appreciative listening, like comprehensive listening, often overlooks facts and issues being communicated. Again, the goal is not to eliminate this or any of the other filters from your toolbox but to improve your ability to perceive the entire range of information and emotions.

EMPATHIC LISTENING FILTER

The final filter is empathic listening. This is the type of listening that takes place between two friends over a cup of coffee. This is the process of listening with the intent to support the speaker. Mental health professionals use this type of listening in therapy. However, it isn't confined to the behavioral health profession.

Anyone who listens to help, support, or empathize with the speaker is using this type of listening skill.

Executive coaches help professionals move through roadblocks in their careers by listening empathically to the client's story. This enables them to revise their own future in a way that takes into account the roadblocks in their career and empowers them to overcome those obstacles and move forward.

We are wired to listen empathically.

We have mirror neurons in our brains designed to mimic the behaviors and actions we see in those around us. When listening empathically we visualize what we're hearing, so as the speaker relates a story, we will tend to react as if we are experiencing that incident ourselves.

Empathic listening happens every day. You experience an empathic response, all courtesy of your very own mirror

neurons, when someone tells you about an unpleasant experience and you instinctually wince, or you *feel* it in your gut. If you
are a dog lover, and one of your coworkers tells you that a car
hit his pet, you feel it too! That's empathic listening.

It is not acting. It is walking in someone's shoes and feeling the rub of leather on your feet and understanding *why* he
doesn't particularly like that pair of shoes.

We define these five areas as filters because—depending on
our personality type and a host of other variables—we tend to
favor one or more and turn a deaf ear to the others. However,
the skillful listener learns to attend to *all five areas* and maximiz-
es his or her ability to clearly and accurately sense the speaker's
message.

All of us tend to zone in on one particular area over another. This is frequently a difference that falls along gender lines,
as men tend to listen more for facts, while women tend to be
better at hearing the emotional content of the message.

This is not to say that females don't listen for facts or that
men are blind to emotional content. It is just that guys are
more oriented to facts and sometimes oblivious to the emotional content of a conversation.

Remember the old TV show *Dragnet?* The detective would
always say, "Just the facts, ma'am." While females also listen to
facts, they tend to be keenly aware of the emotional content of
a conversation. They are more prone to listen to establish and
verify emotional connection.

There are those who might disagree whether this is a ge-
netic or a socialized difference. Either way, gender-based filtering happens.

In her book, *You Just Don't Understand,* Deborah Tannen observes gender-based filtering is apparent even with very young
children at play. In Tannen's research, she observed that little
boys on the playground communicate to establish their place
in the pecking order. Their play was centered on establishing
their position of domination by determining who's in charge.

Conversations between little boys had to do with establishing their position or rung on the ladder.

Tannen also observed little girls at play were centered on being part of the group and ensuring their connection to the group was alive and well. For little girls, conversation was a means of maintaining emotional connection. This might be a biologically-based issue, regardless of our gender, but we can learn skills to compensate for our deficiencies.

You will begin to fine-tune your ears for better listening. You will be able to understand whether you are focused on facts or emotions, and this will certainly help your ability to sense and process more accurately.

You must also be able to determine when a specific conversation calls for focusing on the facts or emotions being communicated by the speaker. Sometimes the speaker is just trying to convey facts while, at other times, the speaker is conveying emotions. But either way, there is always an underlying emotional message that needs to be perceived, deciphered, and responded to.

Skillful listeners, however, strive to integrate all five of these styles as they focus on the speaker.

PERSONALITY STYLE FILTERS

In the 1920s, researchers determined there are four basic personality styles or ways people interact. This research has evolved into personality surveys such as the Myers-Briggs Type Indicator and the DISC assessment, two among many surveys or indicators that point out differences in the way healthy human beings approach relationships.

These different styles of relating can present their own unique filters with barriers to listening for that particular personality style.

An introvert who is focused on details might have filters that inhibit his or her ability to listen empathically. On the other hand, the extrovert who is not concerned with details or is very relational might have a filter that makes it difficult to hear the details imbedded in the message they are hearing.

It is important to understand males, females, extroverts, introverts, engineers, accountants, salespeople, and driven executives all have unique filters we must be aware of and contend with in order to listen well. So be aware of the four basic personality styles, each with inherent strengths and weaknesses that impact the listener and the speaker.

MOOD FILTERS

Our mood or emotional state can also be a filter.

Did your mom ever ask you if you got up on the wrong side of the bed? The implication is you didn't get a good night's sleep, and you're grumpy about everything. Are you having a bad day, a good day? Whatever emotions you're experiencing at the moment certainly have an impact on how we hear, listen, and react to what we comprehend.

People in recovery from addiction recognize there are times when their emotional state tends to make them prone to relapse. They refer to this as HALT, or hungry, angry, lonely, or tired. If you're suffering from HALT, you need to know that some emotional filter could potentially keep you from accurately hearing the speaker's message.

HEARING WITH YOUR EYES

Sensing is much more than just hearing words without filters. We also listen with our eyes by taking into account the speaker's facial expressions and their body language. We even note how close they are to us as well as the subtle messages that are imbedded between the lines.

Research has shown salespeople who are skilled listeners are acutely aware of the tone of the conversation as well as the mood and emotions of the speaker. For example, in a sales situation, a customer might not specifically say a prompt delivery is important to them. However, their vocal inflection and facial expressions might be clearly saying, "Being delivered by this date is a deal maker." The customer might not literally *say* on-time delivery is an important feature, but the salesperson, engaged in powerful listening, senses this message through the customer's tone of voice and facial expressions.

PROCESSING

All listening begins with sensing. Once information sensing begins, the brain goes about the business of processing the incoming data. This second dimension of listening refers to the cognitive operations going on inside the brain.

Back to the metaphorical camera: when I take a picture, the shutter opens, the camera senses or gathers optical information, and, within a millisecond, begins to process that picture so, an instant later, I can see the results on the screen. During processing, the brain organizes the perceived messages and transforms them into meaningful and usable information and processes it into a picture.

It is important to note that *processing* is not the same as *interpreting*.

Let me use the camera metaphor to clarify this. You take a picture with the camera, but you edit the picture on your computer using Photoshop or some other image-altering program. The goal of processing is to get the clearest and most detailed picture possible, without altering the image.

You are looking at a picture of the outline of a person in a dark alley. You have an image of someone walking down a dark alley and, thus, you have *processed* that picture in your mind. However, you conclude from that picture that he is an escaped convict intent on robbing someone under the cloak of darkness. If so, you have *interpreted* that image and, most likely, drawn a premature conclusion.

Processing is accurately collecting as much information as possible without arriving at a premature conclusion.

The problem with premature conclusions and judgments is they are often incorrect. The difficulty is getting an erroneous notion out of our brain once it has lodged in our neurons. Then the biggest problem is these premature conclusions trigger four behaviors that give rise to unnecessary conflicts: *escalation, invalidation, negative interpretation,* and *withdrawal.*

All of us have experienced escalation. When a misunderstanding occurs, the listener might respond emotionally, raising the level of tension in the conversation. The speaker, feeling further misunderstood, might respond in kind by "upping the ante" and coming right back with a terse comment. Hence, the conversation escalates in a negative way.

The situation between Jill and Brian at the beginning of the chapter is an example of escalation.

You have probably found yourself in a heated argument wondering, "How did our pleasant conversation end up here?" The answer is someone arrived at a premature conclusion, and the conversation escalated into an argument.

The second product of a premature conclusion is negative interpretation. That's where the listener assumes something negative about what they hear without having gotten all the facts. Negative interpretation invariably leads to escalation.

Suppose Jeff buys Jennifer a cup of coffee on his way to work just to be nice. When he gives it to her, she says, "Thanks. Now, what new project are you getting ready to dump in my lap?" Jennifer has just assumed the worst of Jeff's motives. Negative interpretation happens. We are wary of others, and we tend to assume the worst motives to explain their actions until proven otherwise. Having his integrity challenged, Jeff responds in anger, and the conflict begins to escalate.

The third action that comes from a premature conclusion is invalidation, where the listener does not treat as important what they are hearing from the speaker.

For example, you ask your boss for permission to attend special training to improve your skills and enhance your professional image. His or her response is "That's silly. You don't need to take that training...that's just a waste of time and money." You will most likely feel "invalidated." Something very important to you has been deemed unimportant by the listener. This premature judgment will lead to escalation or to withdrawal, the fourth result of premature judgments.

Withdrawal is cutting off the conversation or just "leaving" mentally. If the listener is threatened by what he or she is hearing and gets defensive, their reaction might be to put up defensive walls and emotionally distance themselves from the conversation or even get up and walk out.

Withdrawal triggers deep abandonment issues in many, and is often met with a strong and seemingly irrational response. As a listener, we can appear to be withdrawing when we attempt to carry on the conversation and multitask or try to do something else at the same time.

For fear of losing his job, Brian might not get up and walk out on Jill in the middle of the conversation, but he has withdrawn from the conversation. Mentally, he has already left the building, and listening is not taking place.

Escalation, invalidation, negative interpretation, and withdrawal all begin with premature judgments or conclusions. They are part of a chain reaction that leads to a real meltdown. These four actions tend to fuel a condition called *fight or flight*, the ultimate filter that presents the most formidable barrier to listening and causes many conflicts.

When a person is in fight or flight, they might appear to be unreasonable or irrational. This is caused by a change in the brain when a person feels threatened.

Under normal circumstances, we make decisions, learn new things, and interact with others by using the prefrontal cortex part of the brain. This is our "logical" brain.

However, when we are startled, feel under attack, or worse yet, perceive we're in danger, the lower part of the brain—or, as some call it, the "lizard" brain—takes control. The lizard part of the brain is not logical or good at decision making. It is, however, fast and decisive in order to get us out of harm's way. The problem is when our brain is in fight or flight, *everything* around us feels like an attack. Good conversations don't take place when fight or flight is present. Skillful listening vanishes, only to be replaced by destructive communication. In fight or flight, we say and do things that we would never consider saying or doing in a normal situation.

This is why it is important for the skillful listener to be aware of the importance of listening to understand, listening to get all the content of the message, and listening without jumping to premature conclusions. And what happens when we don't?

Once a premature conclusion is rooted in the mind, a preponderance of evidence to the contrary cannot easily dislodge that notion. Once a conversation escalates to the level of fight or flight, it takes about thirty minutes to calm down and return to normal.

Great listeners do their very best to gather all the facts and are careful not to rush to judgment. They are aware conflict can be managed by the way they process what they are hearing and, only then, they respond in an appropriate manner.

RESPONDING

The final element of skillful listening is the response. It refers to the feedback the listener sends to the speaker to indicate he or she has been heard. When the speaker receives this feedback response, he or she is assured he or she is being understood and is encouraged to continue speaking.

Skillful listening does not happen until the listener makes an appropriate response.

When there is no response at all, the speaker is left wondering whether or not he is getting his point across. Sometimes when speaking to another person on the phone, you might not hear a response and ask, "Are you still there, or did we get disconnected?" It is more difficult but probably just as important to ask that question in person if the person on the listening end has not provided any response to what they have heard.

Almost as bad as no response is the "fix-it" response, where the listener comes up with a solution to the problem he's just heard. Fix-it responses cause invalidation and, again, tend to fuel fight or flight. I can't tell you how many women I've heard say, "I don't want him to fix me. I just want him to listen to me."

There are times when the conversation requires a fix-it response. But, if it can be buffered by a time of just listening to understand, it makes the fixing a lot more palatable and effective.Ultimately, good listeners seek to understand rather than be understood. They respond in a way that says, "I hear what you are saying" and not "I hear, and I know what you need."

The feedback response can take a verbal or nonverbal form. The salesperson using his or her powerful listening skills might show the customer his message is being received by nonverbal signals such as head nods or facial expressions. In addition, the salesperson might use short verbal prompts or pose more explicit questions that probe further into the issue. He or she might ask for more information or seek clarification.

Such nonverbal and verbal factors indicate the message has been received and expedite understanding between both parties to the sales interaction. Responding is important for the sake of the speaker, but it benefits the listener as well.

Researchers have discovered that as the listener's outward responsiveness increases, so does their retention level. In one study, listeners who crossed their arms when they listened retained 38 percent less than listeners who kept their arms at their sides and assumed an "open" body posture.

TYPES OF RESPONSES

We have a number of choices to make when we respond. First, we can choose to *focus* on the speaker's point of view and respond accordingly, or we can respond by stating our own point of view, which invariably alienates us from the speaker. Notice that each of these choices either moves us closer to understanding the speaker or farther apart from the speaker and his or her experience.

Second, we have a choice as to *what* content we respond to, the event or condition, the people involved, or what the speaker's words say about himself or herself. When we respond to the speaker's self-perception, we are moving into his world and truly focusing on his needs and what is most important to him.

Third, we have a choice of *how* to respond by giving our own opinions and facts, or interpreting their words, or asking more questions, or simply accepting and clarifying what we hear. Asking questions and clarifying what we have heard will continue to draw us closer to exactly what the speaker needs to express.

Fourth, there is a choice as to the *level* at which we respond. We can respond to the content of the speaker's words or the feelings that are either expressed or implied by the content of their words. And we can respond to their positive and negative feelings and the ambivalent feelings they express as they speak. By responding to their feelings, we are able to help them get to the bottom of the issue that they are grappling with and trying to resolve.

In the earlier example, Jill was upset because one of her team members was responsible for providing some information for a big meeting. This person did minimal research and provided a report, but it was far less than what the team promised. Jill felt like her teammate's failure to follow through with adequate documentation made Jill look like she was the one who was not prepared for the meeting. Jill is angry. She goes to her boss and expresses her anger.

Her supervisor's first choice of responses may either be: "This sounds serious. Please tell me more," or it might be, "I don't let people get away with doing that sort of thing. You need to do something about this."

His second level of response will focus on either the situation or what Jill is feeling about herself . This response might be, "Everybody knows your coworker is a big jerk, so don't worry about it," or it could be, "This has caused a cascade of problems you believe makes you look bad, and that really bothers you."

The third level of choice, or how to respond, might be either "I think you ought to just drag your feet the next time he asks you for help," or "Jill , what do you think you should do about this?," or "You are really not certain what the best course of action would be, are you?"

The fourth level of responses requires a choice of attending to the content of the speaker's words or the feelings embedded within those words.

This final choice of responses might be either: "You are just mad about the situation; get over it," or "You are really struggling with your own feelings of embarrassment. What do you think you should do about this situation?"

There is an array of choices that require accurate sensing and careful processing in order to produce thoughtful responses. If all these choices for responses make you a little tired, that is exactly why we call this *active* listening.

Jill's anger and premature conclusions became a filter that blocked her from truly listening to Brian. She had already concluded that Brian was not doing his work before she even started the conversation. She *escalated* the situation, *interpreted* Brian's actions in the most negative light, and *invalidated* Brian's viewpoint. Brian, in turn, went into *withdrawal*, and just two minutes into the conversation, both were in *fight or flight*. No skillful listening took place, but a lot of damage to this work relationship did.

Powerful listening opens doors of personal and professional success in life. It always has all three—sensing, processing, and responding—components of listening. Great listeners understand their response can be helpful to the speaker or can shut the speaker down. Powerful listening also makes use of elements from all five types of listening.

Really skilled listeners understand all the elements of listening and utilize all of those critical elements as they focus on the speaker.

For example, you might be a great empathic listener, able to pick up on the emotional content of the words. But you're missing the facts because of poor sensing skills.

Or, you're not making sense of what you're hearing because of poor processing. Your response will probably be inappropriate and will most likely lead to the wrong course of action.

You are great at discriminatory listening, but you are not able to listen appreciatively and give the speaker the benefit of the doubt. You can come across as wary and untrusting making the speaker so uncomfortable he will probably just stop talking.

A balanced approach is required: an approach that enables us to be reminded to sense accurately without impairment, process efficiently, and respond clearly and appropriately.

How do you remember all of this, use all of these skills at the same time, and do all of them well?

You must engage in active listening—responsive, reflective listening—and it must be heartfelt, or empathic.

ACTIVITIES: REHEARSING TO LISTEN

1. As soon as you finish reading this chapter, go find someone to listen to—whether it is your significant other, the teller at the bank, a co-worker, or a complete stranger. Just do it. The sooner you implement rehearsing, you'll do it better. Just focus on everything they are saying.

2. Put a sticky note on your mirror in your bathroom that says, "I am a great listener and will take the time to listen to people today. They are NOT an interruption; they are a gift."

3. As you listen, try to hear the emotions along with the facts.

4. Take time every day this week to find someone to listen to.

As you listen, consider this:

1. What fogs up your lens? What prevents you from sensing accurately?

2. What things get between you and perceiving the speaker's message?

3. Do you focus on the speaker's point of view or respond by expressing your own point of view?

4. Do you focus on the people involved in the story or how the speaker regards himself in this story? Do you focus on stating your own opinion, or simply asking clarifying questions and paraphrasing the speaker's words?

5. Do you back away from discussing the speaker's feelings or do you respond or paraphrase the positive content of the speaker's story while downplaying any negative or ambivalent feelings?

Want to become a better listener?
Volunteer for:
- ☐ A care line or as a community phone contact
- ☐ A local hospice organization
- ☐ A church ministry that uses laypeople to provide supportive care (such as Stephen's Ministry)

Chapter Four

HOW AM I SUPPOSED TO REMEMBER ALL THIS? ACTIVE REFLECTIVE EMPATHIC (*ARE* LISTENING)

"For every problem there is always one solution that is quick, simple, neat, and usually wrong."
Sign in mechanic's shop

Active, reflective, and *empathic* are the three words we use to describe the type of listening we believe is most beneficial in any relationship, especially where the stakes are high and there is a good chance of conflict or even just a misunderstanding. When we began training people how to listen in a deep and powerful way, we needed a simple word or acronym that would remind the listener to strive to effectively engage in the three components of listening and set aside listening filters as he or she focuses on the speaker.

The word we came up with is "ARE" or "ARE listening." As a reminder for improving your listening skills, pause to ask yourself at the onset of any conversation: *ARE you listening?*

ARE listening stands for active, reflective, and empathic listening. It reinforces accurate sensing, processing, and responding. It draws from all five of the listening filters. It is the action of hearing with an understanding of how important intentional listening is, fully engaging all three of these actions simultaneously, and having an awareness of how incredibly powerful this combination can be.

Let's break down ARE listening.

ACTIVE LISTENING

The first element is active listening. There is no such thing as passive listening for skilled listeners. Active listening means taking a very *intentional* role in listening. It requires constant attention and refocusing on the speaker, by shutting out internal and external filters and distractions and continually avoiding the impulse to arrive at premature conclusions.

A great photographer is constantly attentive to keeping the lens of the camera clean and free of obstructions to ensure that sensing remains accurate. So it is with the great listener.

A skilled photographer will focus on the subject in the picture, but he is also always aware of the stuff in the background that could ruin the picture. Have you ever seen a telephone pole in the background or overhead power lines that ruin the composition of an otherwise perfect picture? In the same way, the listener is mindful of the background stuff that can draw his attention away from the speaker and make perception more difficult.

We also refer to this as active processing, because the listener is simultaneously focused on sensing the words, the inflections, the body language, and all the meta-messages between the lines that will either confirm or contradict what the speaker is saying.

This is listening that uses your whole body, because the listener is actively monitoring his or her posture and body language to communicate openness to the speaker.

In addition, active listening is "going there" in your mind. It is listening that visualizes what the speaker is saying. It is seeing a video playing on a screen in your head that corresponds to what you are hearing. This is listening, which clearly says, "I am really hearing you" and combines the five different styles of listening filters. It seeks to gather facts, yet it is discriminative and vigilant for messages between the lines, such as the speaker's body language.

Even while gathering all this information and interpreting, active listening seeks to comprehend while deferring judgment at the same time. No small order!

Active listening combines these different types of listening while at once remaining alert to the emotional messages that are being communicated.

To become a good active listener, one must mindfully practice all of the different types of listening.

At first, it might seem like chewing gum and patting yourself on the head while keeping a different beat with your foot. However, it is a learned skill or procedural type of learning that improves with practice. Just as with learning to drive a car with a standard transmission, what seemed impossible at first became possible as you practiced what you learned. You can, with practice and time, learn to shift, clutch, accelerate, and steer all at once.

When you begin to engage in active listening, don't be shocked if you find yourself physically and emotionally drained afterward. It is hard work because you are not at all passive, and that's precisely why we call it *active*. While it plays a vital role in being a skilled listener, active listening alone is not enough. It requires reflective listening as well.

REFLECTIVE LISTENING

Reflective listening is just that. You *reflect* back to the speaker what you hear them saying. The purpose is not to sound like my friend's African Gray parrot, who repeats word for word what he hears. Instead, your goal is to paraphrase the speaker's words.

When I teach people how to listen reflectively, they will often ask, "Doesn't this sound stilted or fake? Don't people think you are being weird when you do this?" The answer is "No."

The way you become skilled at reflective listening is by *doing it* as often as you can. At first it might feel awkward, but you're the only one who will likely notice.

You'll also discover that it will quickly become a natural part of the way you relate, and even when you tell someone you are going to listen reflectively, they won't notice it. But they will, however, enjoy how it feels to be heard as they audibly register their own words and thoughts reflected back to them.

Reflective listening uses words and phrases in the form of re-statements, body language, and vocalizations—such as *ums*, *ahhs*, *mmms*—to respond to the listener in order to demonstrate that you hear their words, the unspoken message between the lines, and the emotional content of their message. Your response communicates you are perceiving and processing what you are hearing and that you appreciate their thoughts and feelings.

Humans *need* to be heard.

When we engage in reflective listening, we are sending the message *you are heard, you are valuable, and you make a difference* loud and clear.

Human beings respond naturally and immediately to this kind of treatment. For most people the feeling of being heard and understood is so pleasant they seldom stop to analyze what exactly is happening to make them feel that way.

Reflective listening completes the listening cycle. It is the response part of the perceiving, processing, and responding triangle. Reflective listening is a powerful tool for conflict management. A great leader in the counseling field of the twentieth century, Carl Rogers, suggested when in conflict, you should never respond to a statement until you have first "reflected" the speaker's words and emotional content back to them.

One of the benefits of taking the time to do this when experiencing conflict is the process of reflection slows the conversation down and offers the best chance of preventing it from escalating into a heated argument, while you clarify what you think you are hearing. This is the essence of reflection.

Good listeners learn to "reflect" what they hear by paraphrasing the speaker's words. You can become proficient at this by always restating everything you hear before responding. If you practice this every time someone speaks to you, it will soon feel perfectly natural, and you will get to where it is an automatic response. It becomes a subconscious procedural skill you will "do" automatically. You won't need to think through a checklist of things to be effective; you'll just do it instinctively.

EMPATHIC LISTENING

Empathic listening is climbing into the other person's shoes, seeing the world through her eyes, hearing through her ears, and experiencing life and all its trials as she experiences it. If the speaker is happy about what she is relating, you feel happy with her. If she is sad, you might not weep with her, but you truly try to comprehend the emotion she is feeling in that very moment. You are attuned to her emotions.

Empathic listening is when someone tells us about a bad experience he had, and we wince with him; we—to a small extent—vicariously share that particular experience he is relating. In that powerful moment, we clearly communicate, *"You are not alone."* This enables us to connect with other people at a deep level.

Empathic listening is also important for conflict resolution and mediation, as this is the element of hearing and understanding that brings about reconciliation and redeems positive outcomes from negative situations.

However, the empathy must be real in order for this to take place. Empathy is not faked. It must be genuine. Without genuine empathy, good listening simply does not take place.

Nancy Ferrell provided federal government mediation for community race-related conflicts. Ferrell says mediation rarely works if some measure of empathy is not developed between the parties.

She describes a case involving black students and members of a white fraternity that held an annual "blackface" party.

At the outset, the student president of the fraternity was convinced that the annual tradition was harmless and inoffensive. It wasn't until Ferrell, as mediator, created an opportunity for the student president to listen to the aggrieved parties at the table that he realized the pernicious impact his fraternity's antics had on black students.

Once he recognized the problem, a solution to that part of the conflict was easy to resolve.

Before beginning this mediation session, Ferrell was careful to look for clues that the parties would respond to each other with some measure of empathy long before bringing them together.

"One of my decisions about whether they were ready to meet at the table was whether or not I could get any glimmer of empathy from all sides. If I couldn't get some awareness of sensitivity to the other party's position, I was reluctant to go to the table.

"If you can't create empathy, you can't have a relationship. Without that, mediation is not going to work," she says.

Empathy must be present for skillful *ARE* listening to take place.

FOR THE EMPATHICALLY CHALLENGED

Is your personality style or profession centered on dealing with facts, or does your work require critical listening most of the time? If so, reading the emotional content of the message might prove to be difficult for you at first. It might take some time and practice to develop the ability to pick up on the emotional dimension or content of a conversation.

But, if you are reading this book, it's an indication that, at one time in your young life, you learned twenty-six abstract symbols and eventually developed the ability to put them together into groups. You learned each grouping of symbols represented a specific word with a specific meaning, and then you learned hundreds of thousands of these words.

If your mind can do something as complex as reading the words on this page, you can learn to recognize the four or five basic emotions embedded in conversations.

If you live in a world of facts, it is possible to move into the realm of emotions. It might take some time before you become fluent in the language, but there are great rewards for making the effort.

When we become skillful at empathic listening, our ability to respond is vastly improved. When understanding the speaker's feelings and then restating those feelings in an appropriate way becomes our habitual response, we connect with them in a deeper, more powerful way.

I believe when people practice empathic listening, they become more other-centered, sensing, and empathizing. They begin to take on more of the qualities of character that define a good person. When I empathize with others, I see the world through their eyes. I understand them better; I move away from self-centeredness toward other-centeredness, and that in turn makes me a better person.

PUTTING IT ALL TOGETHER

ARE listening or active, reflective, empathic listening, attempts to consciously combine all three components of listening by providing a framework designed to enable the listener to mindfully engage in efficient sensing, processing, and responding in an active and empathic way.

Now, please understand that nobody can listen this way all the time. We all have our moments when our listening skills are not so good—for instance, when I am teaching a seminar on listening, I always tell my participants that they probably won't see me modeling great ARE skills when I conclude a training session. After I have been training a group all day, I go into the "blind stares" for a while as I unwind from my adrenaline high.

We can't possibly be totally focused all the time. However, we will eventually find ourselves using all of these three skills naturally and with ease the more we attempt to employ them every time we need to listen to someone else. In the following chapters we will explore some simple actions that will trigger the reminder to listen using the ARE skills whenever you engage in conversation with others.

As with spelling and grammar rules we memorize, other actions allow our body to memorize certain activities, such as learning to play the piano and keyboarding, because they involve repetitive physical actions. Pilots, police officers, and firefighters memorize complex operations by doing them over and over.

This is a protocol. We repeat these actions until we do them without even having to think about what we are doing. The importance of practicing a protocol until it becomes a body memory is that we will carry out that memorized action even under unexpected or adverse conditions.

Pilots practice landing by doing "touch-and-go" exercises until they can land a plane without thinking. This is valuable when the unexpected happens, such as being on final approach and hitting a sudden wind sheer. If caught off guard—even if they are panicked—they can continue to carry out the steps to a safe landing, because the memory is so engrained in their mind and body that they retain clarity of purpose even in an emergency situation. Their hands know what to do even when their brain is confused.

Conflict can break out unexpectedly any time. If you have not practiced ARE listening, you might easily find yourself in an escalating conflict. However, if you have practiced slowing yourself down and listening in this powerful and mindful fashion, you have a better chance of ending the conversation on a positive note because the skill is second-nature.

There are times when you can't pick up a pamphlet and remind yourself, "Now this is the way I'm supposed to listen." Life has a nasty way of imposing on us without checking our calendar or to-do list to see if we're up to the task at that moment.

So how is ARE listening different from other forms of active listening? It isn't so much a matter of how different it is. It's just more complete. You can listen actively without listening empathically. You can listen empathically without reflecting. You can really listen closely and process what you hear without responding empathically.

Law enforcement and first responders must do this very exercise on a daily basis. In their line of work, they must get all the facts, but if they get drawn in to the emotional content, they are headed for burnout.

You can really feel what someone is saying without giving any response to his or her words. ARE listening reminds you to do all these at the same time, as much as is possible.

The point of ARE listening is to bring the very best skills to the table and combine them into one powerful tool where sensing, processing, and responding all take place.

HOW I CAME TO SEE THE IMPORTANCE OF THIS

If you will recall, I came to see the importance of powerful, or ARE, listening from my experience as a counseling therapist. I will never forget my graduate school professor's admonition, "If you listen to people and attentively follow their story, they will find the solution on their own."

As a beginning therapist, I would at times find myself lost and confused about what to do to help the client, who was at that moment pouring his or her heart out in the counseling session. That professor's words were often the compass that gave me direction and actually allowed me to help the client.

I would simply return to powerful listening and find that within a few moments, the client would respond, the real issue would come to the surface, and the session would take a turn toward providing a powerful and healing experience for the client—all this by merely listening. The worst thing, I found, was when I got ahead of the client and didn't listen to them and then deluded myself into thinking I actually knew what they needed.

Remember the tendency to arrive at a premature conclusion? We make a big mistake anytime we assume we know what the other person needs, or wants, when we draw those conclusions without listening. That same professor always said that when we *assume* it makes an *ass* out of *u* (you) and *me*. When we jump ahead to those premature conclusions, we are more prone to engage in advice-giving or comparing stories, or any number of inappropriate reactions.

The most dramatic example of the power of ARE listening is in mending troubled relationships. Many couples come to therapy as a last-ditch effort to save a marriage.

The method that seemed to work best for me is the counseling model previously mentioned, developed by researchers from the University of Denver, called PREP® (Prevention and Relationship Enhancement Program). It's simple, easy to remember, and focuses on teaching couples in troubled relationships how to listen to each other. It helps a couple in conflict to understand, recognize, and avoid the four behaviors that destroy good listening and spawn conflict.

What makes this method work so well is its simplicity. It just *intuitively* makes sense. Helping couples in volatile relationships is one of the most difficult endeavors in counseling, but the PREP method worked well.

I often witnessed an immediate softening when an angry spouse began to use ARE listening. You could see the antagonism drain from their partner's face only to be replaced with compassion and understanding. I wondered, "If this tool works in the most difficult of relationships, why couldn't it work in the marketplace and in other relationships that don't require as much of a full-time commitment as marriage?" That inspired me to move into providing these same services in business.

As I developed workshops for dealing with conflict in the workplace, I found that those same principles *did* work, and participants validated my own conclusions.

WHEN THERE IS NO SOLUTION

It would be nice if every problem in the world could be fixed with a balanced scorecard approach, an insightful project manager, a few coaching or counseling sessions, a great brainstorming session, or with just the right combination of actions. The sad truth is that about 80 percent of all relationship problems actually have *no* solution. That is a pretty grim statistic, unless you understand the one issue that makes the 80 percent a lot better is when people feel *heard.*

When ARE listening is used in a problem situation, just being heard is often the solution. How frequently have I heard a wife turn to her husband during counseling and say, "I don't need you to fix me. Just listen to me."

The customer service person who understands this concept will be successful at turning unhappy calls into repeat customers by just providing a listening ear to someone who feels as if he didn't get what he paid for.

Mediation is an area where ARE listening is particularly effective in solving problems. All leaders, managers, and supervisors are mediators from time to time. Your ability to listen, mediate, and lead others to listen to each other when stakes are high is directly connected to your success.

THE ESSENCE OF ARE LISTENING

The essence of ARE listening is actively engaging in the process of frequently stopping the bus of life, getting off, and taking the time to focus on another human being. It is not acting. It is sincere. It is not seeing people as just another sale, or someone from whom I can benefit. ARE listening is not some secret weapon to get what I want from others.

Instead, it is seeing people as unique creations in the universe with stories to tell that are fascinating because of their uniqueness. It is hearing their stories and resonating with them. It is providing some deep sort of connection in that moment. It is saying with all your being, "You are the most important thing in my life at this particular moment," and believing this is not a random chance encounter. Powerful listening is learning to like people and learning to look for, and find, the very best in each person.

HOW IT WORKS

The first step is to simply begin to listen attentively when presented with the opportunity. Just getting a picture of a more patient, more focused, more attentive *you* in your mind is the best place to begin the journey.

Rehearsing to listen is getting up in the morning and visualizing yourself listening to those who have been put in your path on this day. Rehearsal, or practice, is what you do to improve a skill. ARE listening is simply a skill that you will master with time. Rehearsing, practicing, and visualizing this skill will not only change your hearing, it changes your vision as well because you will begin to *see* people differently.

The process of listening deeply moves us from our little world into another person's universe. It causes us to see the person who rides our bus to and from work every day a little differently. It reminds us that people around us are not just objects or cogs in a machine. Instead we begin to see them as human beings with great value, unique stories, loves, hopes, and fears. We give them an opportunity to come alive when we take the time to listen to them, and in the process we become more human, more caring, and more focused on others.

WHAT IT'S NOT

As I have coached people in ARE listening, I have often heard this objection: "Won't it sound like I'm admitting I actually *did* something wrong if I am listening to someone vent or complain about something I have done, and I paraphrase their words back to them?"

ARE listening is not the same as *agreeing* with the other person. It is demonstrating that you truly hear and understand the other person. You can engage in ARE listening in a conflict with someone who is angry with you and reflect his or her words and emotions back without agreeing or implicating yourself, because this is not the same thing as an admission or confession of guilt, nor is it a demonstration of weakness.

Moreover, when people engage in ARE listening, they win the respect of their opponent and are more likely to come to a solution. The opponent is often much more predisposed to listen once he or she feels heard.

"Aren't you just encouraging people to vent and gripe?" is another objection I have encountered. Or, "I don't have time to listen to my employees whine or talk about how they feel." I'm not suggesting you spend hours upon hours listening to someone vent.

What I *am* suggesting is in those moments where you *must* listen to your employees, you should listen skillfully, to the very best of your ability, because you don't have time *not* to listen. Consider the cost of recruiting, interviewing, and training a replacement after that employee has left your business. Remember, employees don't leave a job; they leave a boss they believe doesn't appreciate or listen to them.

WHAT IT DOES

Daniel Siegel, a well-known researcher and neuroscientist, has made great contributions to the study of the brain and psychology. In his book, *The Developing Mind,* he describes a process that occurs when two human beings are engaged in deep conversation. He states the human mind is something that moves beyond the confines of the brain, the head, and the body, and it is energized and actualized when it connects with other minds. This occurs when that person is truly heard and understood. We want to demonstrate the tremendous power that is unleashed when this takes place.

YOU NEED THIS!

Powerful listening is a skill that anyone *can* learn and everyone *should* learn. It is not just for psychotherapists and CEOs. If you are a hermit and live alone in a cave, you are probably the only person who doesn't need to improve your listening skills. Being able to smell does not require lessons, but being able to distinguish the delicate nuances between different fragrances and perfumes requires training. Being able to listen might not require lessons either, but to engage in powerful, skillful listening that leads to success does require learning new skills and consistent practice.

ACTIVITIES: LISTENING FOR A LOT MORE

1. Listen for facts as well as the feelings behind the facts.

2. Identify the speaker's main points with a key word or phrase.

3. Take brief notes while you listen.

4. Constantly summarize the speakers' previous points by repeating key words in your mind.

5. Rehearse in your mind how you will listen to others.

Chapter Five

HOW *NOT* TO LISTEN

"Big egos have little ears."
Robert Schuller

THE JOYS OF BEING A GOLF VIRGIN

I am one of the few people in my circle of friends who has never played a single round of golf. I don't have anything against the game. In fact, the thought of riding around a pristinely manicured golf course in a quiet little electric golf cart with good friends and cute girls bringing cold beverages on a warm summer day sounds pretty good!

It's just that I have never taken the time to learn how to play.

My good friend, the golf pro, is dying to get me out on the greens and teach me how to play. Why? Because I am the "ideal" student. I don't have a bunch of bad habits he would have to undo. Here I am: clay in the sculptor's hands, pliable and ready to be made into a masterpiece, or a master golfer.

Apparently much of his frustration comes from students who are self-taught, or just badly taught, who show up for their first lesson with years of poor habits that need to be fixed before he can begin the joy of teaching the game of golf.

So it is with listening.

Before one can become a skillful listener, they must first deal with faulty listening habits. I have known professionals who excel in their careers in every way except for their listening skills. A lot of them listen poorly, and these habits have a huge impact on their work.

While they might be successful *despite* their inability to listen, they could certainly enhance their effectiveness and success by improving their listening skills. I often wish I could just shadow them for a few days and coach them on the art of what to do. I'm confident I could radically improve their effectiveness as professionals.

The first order of business for tapping into the incredible power of listening is to check for poor listening and begin to break away from those behaviors that prevent us from really hearing others. Becoming aware of and correcting those practices first clears the way to learning more effective ways of listening.

SIX BAD HABITS

When I think of poor listening skills, I see a mental picture of friends and associates I have known who have had one or more of the following "don'ts" that keep us from really listening.

Everyone who wants to become a better listener needs the counterpart of the golf pro—a listening coach—who can help break his bad habits so he can begin to build good ones.

Most can't afford a listening coach to be a constant shadow for a week or two. But, if you have a like-minded friend who also wants to improve his or her listening skills, you could recruit him or her to be your listening partner.

Consider asking your significant other to help you improve your listening skills by pointing out whenever you're guilty of any of the following six habits.

You need to be aware of them and how they might show up in your listening style, because they need to be addressed before you can learn how to listen well.

They are:

1. Nonstop talking
2. Planning what to say next
3. Frequent interrupting
4. Looking away often
5. Never asking clarifying questions
6. Forming hasty conclusions or opinions

1. Nonstop talking

You've heard the joke about the narcissist who says, "Enough about me, let's talk about you...what do you think about me?" The irony is that you don't have to be a narcissist to fall into this. Most people don't like long silent pauses in conversations. Those lapses of chatter make us feel uncomfortable, so we fill up the dead air with words.

The next time you are in a conversation, monitor your own speech and be aware of the amount of time you are speaking. Talking too much is an easy hazard to get stuck in, because it is easier to go on about yourself and what you are interested in. Let's face it, talking about ourselves is what we do best! After all, we're so interesting!

Beyond just talking more than listening, there is the obsessive behavior of the pathological talker—the person who talks nonstop and never comes up for air. The pathological chatterbox might well be someone who just grew up an only child, or a nervous child, or just a child with an active mind. They can talk about anything, anytime.

Most pathological talkers are not aware of just how much they monopolize the conversation, even though they might make self-deprecating comments from time to time about their own need to constantly talk.

Do you have concerns that you might be a pathological talker? Do you fear that every now and then you talk more than you should? Again, the secret is to monitor your own conversations like a third-party quality-control agent.

The next time you have a meeting, go to a party, or have lunch with a friend or associate, consider taking a few minutes before your meeting and visualizing how you'd like that conversation to unfold in your mind.

Rehearse listening more and speaking less and arm yourself with an inquisitive and curious mind. Ask questions and get the other person started. Then, do your part by visualizing yourself doing a lot more listening.

Imagine yourself being comfortable with breaks in the conversation. See yourself looking for opportunities to ask questions that would encourage the speaker to freely express his or her thoughts and feelings.

Prepare yourself to be OK with moments where the conversation lapses into silence, and steel yourself to not rush into making conversation. Rather, just accept that in any given conversation there is ebb and flow. Sometimes the silences give someone the opportunity to form his thoughts or to summon up the courage to say something that is really on his mind.

The way you break the "just keep talking" habit is by finding ways to remind yourself to limit your talking. This is accomplished by focusing intently on what the other person is saying.

Remember, powerful listening is composed of clear sensing, accurate processing, and effective responding. If you're talking nonstop, you can't do *any* of these very well.

2. Planning what you are going to say next

While you are *not* talking, you can either focus on what the other person is saying, or you can be thinking of what you are going to say next.

Most of us think four times faster than the other person can speak, so thinking ahead, planning a response, or making a mental shopping list are easy to do.

I am in deep trouble if I use the other person's speaking time as a pit stop for me to plan my response, review my week, or plan my next sales call.

You see, when I am faking listening, it shows on my face like one of those LED billboards that have high definition. The speaker will instantly know that while the lights are still on, you have definitely left the building. We all want to take part in the conversation and we want to keep up with the discussion at the table. But planning our next words while the other person is speaking will not win us any points. It just comes across as phony, and everybody sees it.

When this habit is lurking about, conversations often become one-up matches, where everyone is competing to make the best point, like a bunch of guys having pizza and cold beer while trying to out-do each other's tall tales. The conversation rapidly evolves into a one-up fest.

It might feel great in the moment, because I was able to say the coolest thing, tell the most unusual story, or give the best play-by-play analysis of last week's football game. But in the long run, I will *not* win friends, influence people, or be thought of as the life of the party.

In my professional training seminars, I invite participant interaction, but I have to keep a tight rein on my own brain in order to remain focused in the moment and not go planning what I am going to say next.

What is the antidote to the tendency to think about what you are going to say next? Make yourself slow down, focus on the speaker's words, and learn to "be in the moment." You need to be all there when you're there. It's simply good sense. It's a habit that will not only make you a better listener but will also draw people to you. It will make you more patient, and you'll probably live longer too.

Before your next conversation, take a few minutes to visualize yourself being in the moment with the speaker. See yourself letting go of any agenda of things you want to say and just going with the other person, allowing her to take the conversation where she needs to go. Get a mental picture of yourself intently focused on her words.

When we have a clear picture of ourselves doing a specific behavior, we are able to make that behavioral change much more quickly. See yourself caught up in the other's story and remember, "It's not about me, it's about them."

3. Frequent interrupting

Now here is a bad habit that will eventually shut the other person down—interrupt the conversation with topics that are tangential or completely off the subject. The stopping and starting will wear the speaker down to the point she'll just give up and think "why bother; I'll just shut up."

Interrupting frequently can be jumping in to finish what the other person is saying. Often people who interrupt mean well. They think they are demonstrating good listening skills by showing the person they are on the same page, but it doesn't work that way. Instead, the speaker will just stop talking.

Beware especially of the well-intentioned "I know just what you mean. That same thing happened to me" response. It is easy to think that matching someone's story with a similar experience is relating to what she is saying and empathizing with it.

But to the speaker, it can feel like the listener has engaged in a game of "one-up." Instead, she tends to hear, "You think you've got it bad—well, listen to what happened to me." Or it comes across as "I can top that story." The exasperated person's natural response to that statement is "Nothing I experience is all that big a deal. Why should I even bother to talk?"

Interruptions are like driving in rush-hour traffic. Stops, starts, accelerating, and then braking quickly wear out the engine of conversation. What you want instead is to encourage relational motion and flow by keeping others in speaking mode.

When I eat at a fine restaurant, I like to read the entire menu before I make up my mind what to order. If I am halfway through reading the menu and someone asks me a question or speaks to me, I have to go back up to the top and start all over. For some reason, my brain needs that uninterrupted perspective before I can make up my mind.

Some people are like that in conversations. If we would just be quiet and give them a chance, they would really say what is actually on their mind. When we interrupt, it forces them to start all over.

Before your next conversation, visualize yourself monitoring the number of interruptions you are making. When you do engage in conversation, take a moment to clear up of the "housekeeping" things and get the side-road issues settled so you can listen without interruption.

If I am having a business meal and someone wants to get into a deep conversation, I try to get my meal ordered and take care of any pending issues that are at hand, so I can focus on that person without extraneous issues that might cause me to interrupt his or her thoughts.

The other issue in frequent interruptions is the excitement factor. When I am really tracking what a person is saying, it is easy to cut in and finish his sentence or throw in an off-topic idea that was stimulated by something he said.

To counter this, I try to monitor my own level of involvement. When I find that I have gotten ahead of the speaker and interrupted him, I correct myself by holding out my hand as if to pause him, stop the conversation, and interrupt—yes, I said interrupt—and apologize for having interrupted his train of thought. By doing this, it reinforces what I need to do and restores my awareness of how quickly I can forget what I am supposed to know *and* do.

The interrupting habit can be broken, but it often creeps back, especially if we are really passionate about the topic and can relate to what the person is saying. The best way to put an end to this is when you find yourself interrupting, stop, apologize, and resolve to do better next time.

There is something about pausing to acknowledge your mistake to the speaker that tends to reinforce proper behavior and extinguish this tendency in a hurry.

4. Looking away often

When our youngest son was a little boy and needed behavior modification, we would take him aside, sit down, and have a face-to-face talk with him. If he was in *real* trouble and we were having that come-to-Jesus talk, he would do everything he could to avoid eye contact.

I would sit face to face with him, gently cradle his chin in my hands to keep him facing me, and look him in the eye. He would roll his eyes up and away as far as he could to avoid the confrontation. Now, he was just a little guy and that was his way of getting off the hot seat. When I tried to see the world through his eyes, I imagined that he was thinking something like "If I can't beam up and out of here, I'm at least going to treat myself to an out-of-body experience."

As adults, we are just as guilty of zoning out, only we're a lot better at concealing our avoidance or distraction. We look at our watches, our phones, our hands, the artwork on the wall, people coming and going, a good-looking person walking down the street, or the myriad of other attention-stealers.

Our focus is often on everything *but* the person who is speaking. That person might not call attention to our behavior, but you can be sure she will notice it.

Since this—as with every habit—is a learned behavior, it can be replaced with a new habit. Sometimes our distraction is just our body, honestly expressing disinterest in the other person. If you're feeling bored in conversation, your body will probably betray your true feelings. Monitor them, and this will enable you to put a check on getting distracted. If you are bored, just refocus on the speaker.

If you're a person who has difficulty looking others in the face, you need to ask yourself, "What is going on that makes this so difficult?" My training and career as a therapist prompts me to wonder, "What is the deeper hidden issue here?" Fear of intimacy? Discomfort with people? Attention Deficit Disorder? Boredom? All the above?

If you have a hard time looking people in the eyes when listening to them, you might try this simple activity. Find a time when you can sit down, clear your mind, and write. Don't do this on the keyboard. Write out in longhand on a piece of paper in big print: "I don't like to look people in the eyes when I listen to them because_____" and just write down on paper what comes to your mind.

Don't settle for just one answer but keep on brainstorming, and write what comes to your mind, whether it is valid or invalid. Write both the silly and the serious, and chances are you will come up with some statements that when you think them through, you'll find the truth lurking inside. Whatever comes up, target that thought and consider facing whatever it is that comes between you and connecting with others.

The next time you are planning to have a conversation with someone, remind yourself of how you want to challenge that old belief, and change.

If you are having a conversation with a close friend, tell him or her that you want to be better at looking people in the eye when they are talking, and ask him or her to help you with this. Ask him or her to tell you if he or she catches you looking away. Remember habits that are learned are also habits that can be retrained or changed.

5. Never asking clarifying questions

Shouldn't I be quiet and listen? If I ask a question, isn't that interrupting? If you are thinking, "He just told me not to interrupt, and now he's telling me to interrupt," you are partially right. I don't actually want you to interrupt the speaker, but when he pauses to take a breath—and he will—use that moment to ask a clarifying question. This type of question ensures that you are on the same path as the speaker.

It is amazing how often the speaker can be saying one thing, and we really think we are following his thought process, yet we are actually drifting further from the meaning the speaker is attempting to convey.

My favorite musical is *Fiddler on the Roof*, which is about a Jewish community in Russia during the revolution in the early 1900s. The main character, Tevye, has five daughters who are all approaching the marrying age. One evening the local butcher asks him over for vodka because he has something on his mind. He intends to ask for permission to propose to one of his daughters. Tevye, who is the village milkman, is under the impression that the butcher wants to buy his milk cow.

The conversation begins with the butcher commenting on the weather, then asking about his relatives in America, and then, assuming that Tevye knows that he wants to ask for his daughter's hand in marriage, the butcher tells him how fond he is of her. All the time, Tevye thinks he is trying to work up the courage to make an offer on his milk cow. The conversation continues until the butcher says, "I really want her." Irritated, Tevye asks why, to which the butcher replies, "Because I'm lonely." In exasperation Tevye asks, "What are you talking about? How can a little cow keep you from being lonely?" To that the butcher replies, "Is that what you call her, a little cow? I'm talking about your *daughter!*"

Conversations can start off on the same page. We can assume we know what the speaker is saying, and actually we find ourselves far off course. Never assume you understand everything the speaker is saying. If you do, you will be thinking "little milk cow" when the speaker is talking about marriage.

To prevent that drift between what the speaker is saying and what you are actually hearing, take a moment when the speaker pauses and ask something like "Are you saying...?" or "What does this term mean?" If you are confused, hold up your hand—palm facing the speaker the way a police officer stops traffic—and say, "I need to clarify this..." or simply say, "Tell me more about..."

If you are from the United States and you are having a conversation with someone from Great Britain, you need to remember that these are two countries divided by the same language. If you are talking about the boot, you might be thinking about something you put on your feet to go hiking. They might be thinking about a location in an automobile. You might ask for a room to hang your coat and find yourself directed to the bathroom.

Don't assume the obvious. Make it a habit to *not* assume anything and, instead, ask those clarifying questions to keep the picture clear and accurate in your mind as you listen to the other person. This is the one time they will appreciate an interruption, because it says "I am so interested in what you are saying I want to make sure I get it right!"

Develop a curiosity about those around you, especially the person speaking to you.

My mother used to say, "Don't ask questions. It's nosy." I have never felt angry when a friend has asked me a personal question. Instead, I feel cared for.

On the other hand, there have been times in my life when I wished someone had said, "Hey, how are you doing...now really, tell me honestly how are you doing right now."

So don't be afraid to ask those probing questions.

If the listener is uncomfortable with your questions, he or she will probably let you know. With words or body language, you'll get a clear picture if he or she is feeling any discomfort at all.

6. Forming quick opinions and hasty conclusions

The final bad habit to be broken before learning how to listen is forming quick opinions *before* you have heard the entire story. We draw conclusions before we have heard all the facts. Our brains are designed to fill in the gaps.

We engage in a sort of verbal "Wheel of Fortune" game, where we can name what the other person is saying in two letters. Sadly though, we don't score many points even when we are right, which incidentally doesn't happen very often. Most of the time, this habit keeps us off the scoreboard altogether.

Forming quick opinions before we've heard all the facts might make us feel really smart on the rare occasion that we are actually right.

More often than not, however, that quick opinion will have been formed before the speaker has gotten to the most important point in the conversation, and we will miss out on, or minimize, what she was really trying to say.

The way to break this habit is by playing the Nike commercial in reverse: *just don't do it!*

Here again, the way to put a stop to bad habits is by rehearsing ahead of time how you want to see yourself in your next important conversation. Picture yourself listening. As those little bullet points that are forming opinions begin to gather like storm clouds in your brain, see yourself banishing them. Visualize yourself refusing to allow them to cross your mind. Keep telling yourself, "I am going to wait until I hear the entire story *before* I form an opinion."

Those with analytical minds might have a little more trouble breaking this habit, but the key is to remind yourself to hear and make sure you understand the entire story before you arrive at a conclusion.

BREAKING BAD HABITS

Consider establishing a weekly standing appointment with a friend or colleague. Go somewhere quiet, have coffee, and spend an hour coaching each other. Each party takes twenty minutes just to "talk" about whatever is on his or her mind. Both the speaker and the listener should have a list of the six bad habits handy. If the speaker notices the listener displaying one of the taboo behaviors, he or she should gently bring it to the listener's attention or write it down. Both should take a turn listening and speaking. As simple as this seems, it can be a powerful exercise in breaking bad habits and replacing them with a foundation for great listening skills.

Habits are difficult to break because with each of them, our brain has created a neuron path and reinforced those connections that make us respond a certain way without thinking about it. When we attempt to break a habit, we will often fail.

We begin to create a new neural connection that makes a new, good habit possible by recognizing that we failed and by getting back up and consciously altering our behavior after failing.

It is as simple as getting rid of an unwanted path on your front lawn. If people have worn a trail by taking a shortcut across your property, you get rid of the trail they've made by preventing them from using that route any longer. You create an alternate path, break up the soil under the old path, and you plant new grass seeds. Then you water, fertilize, wait, and, in the meanwhile, you encourage trespassers to find a different route. This is the simple picture of changing old habits.

However, there is a deeper component in many of our bad listening habits that makes change difficult: being self-centered.

As infants we have one way of getting what we want: we cry. Babies also have a hard time deferring gratification and satisfaction. *We want what we want, and we want it now!* This is self-preservation for a child but, for an adult, it is just plain selfish.

As a consequence of this, we grow up believing the world revolves around us and, in many ways, we remain that way over our lifetime.

Part of the difficulty of breaking poor listening habits is while they are actions that get us what we want, we continue doing them to meet our own needs without regard for how they affect those around us.

Self-centeredness impacts our ability to listen because it's a lot more fun to talk. Talking brings us pleasure and relieves our pain, and it is a lot more pleasurable to talk about and do things that have to do with "me!" Let's face it, we like ourselves—what we are doing, thinking, and feeling.

The habits of poor listening are a lot easier to change once we face our own flaw of self-centeredness. When I begin to remind myself that it is *not* all about me, it is a lot easier to simply listen to the other person.

Breaking bad habits is much easier when we get over ourselves.

A minister wrote a self-help book on finding purpose in life in forty days. He begins his book with one powerful sentence: "It is not about you." It would be good to remind ourselves of that when we begin to live by this principle and focus on others, even without being coached or taught powerful listening skills. We become better listeners when we begin to look beyond self and see others as important, unique, and fascinating human beings, each having a compelling story to tell.

I have a friend who uses the word "fascinate" in an uncommon way: he says that the key to success is learning to *fascinate* on your work, your world, and what you do. Look for all the interesting things about what you do. You will enjoy your work, and you'll never experience boredom. Apply this to listening. We need to *fascinate* on people.

We are able to drop the bad habits when we approach people with this mindset and *fascinate* on others. We are ready to learn to listen like a pro.

ACTIVITIES: REHEARSING TO LISTEN

1. Before your next conversation, visualize yourself monitoring the amount of interruptions you are making. When you do engage in conversation, take a moment to take care of the housekeeping things and get the side-road issues settled so you can listen without interruption.

2. Take some time to brainstorm this:
   I have trouble looking people directly in the eyes because_____.

3. Consider establishing a weekly standing appointment with a friend or colleague. Go somewhere quiet, have coffee, and spend an hour coaching each other. Each party takes twenty minutes just to "talk" about whatever is on his or her mind. Both the speaker and the listener should have a list of the five habits of bad listeners. The speaker has the floor. If he notices the listener displaying one of the behaviors not to do, he then would gently bring it to the listener's attention or write it down. Both would take a turn listening and speaking.

4. Consider your conversations each day. Review in your mind if and when you were guilty of one of the six bad habits.

5. Get a listening buddy. Spend an hour each week having coffee. Each talks about anything and everything he or she wants to talk about. The other listens for thirty minutes. Reverse roles.

6. Get a trusted friend or loved one to give you an honest assessment of your own listening style and possible bad habits you might have.

7. Make an action plan to break those habits.

8. Become aware of the time you spend talking vs. listening.

Self-evaluation:
What poor listening habits do you struggle with? Write on the back of a business card the one you are most frequently guilty of doing. Write on that same card: "I will learn to…." and read it every morning. See yourself doing just the opposite.

Chapter Six

BEGIN WITH PATIENCE

**"The two most powerful warriors
are patience and time."**
Leo Tolstoy

INTRUSION

I'm working at my computer. The phone rings. My oldest son is calling me to tell me he has set a sales record for the week. I am in the middle of balancing my electronic checkbook, and stopping while crunching numbers always makes me crazy.

I answer. I am kind, but I am not—at this particular moment—patient. I am writing a chapter on listening patiently, and *I* can't even get it right with my own son. Not always.

This is one of my impatient moments. I steel myself and recall the words of a Harry Chapin song about a dad who never had time for his little boy. The song ends with the father reflecting that the boy eventually grew up and became just like him. Distracted and impatient...this is something I *don't* want to pass along to my son. So, after a quick attitude adjustment, I settle down to give him the time he needs. Then after a little while,

I find myself drawn into the moment, the celebration of his success, and before long I no longer have to *make* myself listen patiently. Suddenly I find that I *am* listening patiently.

I wish I could say that it was that way from the beginning of the call. But, this time, I caught myself and pulled out of a nose-dive. The lyrics of the song are a good reminder of the price we pay for always being in such a hurry.

Good listening starts with patience, and my quest is to be a patient listener 100 percent of the time. If I hit 90 percent, I will remind myself that's better than 80 percent, but I'm going for continuous improvement over my lifetime. That's my goal. I want 100 percent!

WHAT DOES IT MEAN TO LISTEN PATIENTLY?

Executive and life performance coaching is a growing industry worldwide. Coaches have helped many people find direction and success in life. At the very heart and soul of good coaching is patient listening.

The coach approaches the client with the belief that the client is creative, resourceful, whole, and instinctively and subconsciously knows where he or she needs to go. Listening patiently on the part of the coach is the key that unlocks the client's energy and potential. Life coaches call this action "being in the moment" or "dancing in the moment." Simply put, this is extremely patient listening or being "totally present."

Something about perceiving, processing, and responding while exuding patience and serenity is the single most important tool that a life coach has at his or her disposal. The coach patiently listens to the client without agenda or preconceived notion of *how* the client needs to resolve his or her dilemma. It is the process of *not* counting the steps or technically analyzing any movement but just *joining* the other person in a dance of self-discovery.

As life coaches, we don't get them there by leading, making them focus on the moves, or telling them *how* to move. We allow them to take the lead, and we learn to merely be with them as a partner in the movement of the moment.

The guiding belief behind this approach is that the person already has the answer somewhere deep inside. The act of patient listening creates a safe place for that answer to make its way to the surface. Coaches and therapists who don't listen patiently tend to jump ahead and invariably impose their own opinions on the client. This action often causes the client to shut down.

We will miss the very essence of what is important to the client when we assume we already know what the client needs. This is an attitude often born out of impatience on our part. Something that appears to be little and insignificant to us might actually be something life-changing to the other person. Psychologists often recount sessions in which the client makes a great discovery or gains that life-altering insight. Ironically, these are not moments when the therapist has made some brilliant therapeutic intervention. Usually, they result from just listening patiently and attentively.

Watching a video of a life coach or therapist listening patiently will show you someone who is following the speaker.

Look into their mind. You will see them resisting the urge to formulate a response to what is being said and working to put all distractions out of their mind. Listen to their internal world. You will hear them reminding themselves that this is the most important task they have in this moment, and this person deserves their full and undivided attention. Also, you will notice they don't interrupt the speaker, nor do they "wait" for a good opportunity to jump in and add their two cents.

Patient listening is more than just setting aside my agenda and just going with the speaker to wherever they need to go. Patient listening is *not* having an agenda and waiting on the speaker to decide where he or she needs to go. More than just a change of behavior, it is a choice to pursue a change in lifestyle. To do this requires a commitment on the part of the listener to cultivate an attitude of patience.

Any career that requires interaction with other humans could benefit from learning to listen patiently the way a therapist or life coach listens. Make this a lifetime pursuit.

COMPONENTS OF PATIENT LISTENING

We hope to provide a clear and concise picture of patient listening by breaking it down into three components. These are following the speaker, valuing the speaker, and respecting the speaker. When exercised consistently, these components enhance patient listening.

PATIENT LISTENING FOLLOWS THE SPEAKER

Patient listening follows the speaker. This is achieved by adopting a mindset in which the listener constantly *chooses* to follow, rather than lead, the conversation. It is more than just listening without interruption.

At the core of patient listening is a shift in the way we regard people around us. It requires understanding that they don't need us to get ahead of them and take them by the hand and lead them through their thought process.

We must begin to see them as competent and somehow instinctually able to know where they need to go and then accept that they don't need our advice or comments, just our presence.

The technique of following the speaker requires—especially for those easily distracted—a mental discipline of continually turning away from distractions and from the temptation to get out ahead of the speaker and tell them where he needs to be headed. We must stay behind the speaker but not so far behind that we lose sight of where they're going.

One side note: Aren't you glad people really can't read our minds? Aside from getting caught in an embarrassing thought, I often wonder what else people might see going on in our heads as they speak. What would they see? Would it be "I am intrigued by what I hear" or "I wish this person would just hurry up and shut up!"

PATIENT LISTENING VALUES THE SPEAKER

Patient listening regards the speaker with supreme value and uniqueness. We are willing to wait for service, for example, or on people we consider important. If I'm leaving for Europe on vacation and the plane is thirty minutes late, I don't leave the airport and cancel my vacation over a little delay, because it is important to me. On the other hand, I may consider going somewhere else to eat if I want a hamburger but there is a thirty-minute wait to get a seat. The difference lies in the importance we place on that particular experience.

We confer high priority and worth on whoever is speaking when we strive to engage in patient listening. We do this by learning to see people as wonderful, unique creations.

The word "snowflake" is often linked to the phrase "no two are alike." In order to value those we listen to, we must see them as real people, and no two are alike, each with a unique story to tell.

The way we value the speaker has more to do with changing the way we regard humanity than merely learning a new technique. Learning to love people and delight in their stories opens the door for patient listening.

PATIENT LISTENING DOES NOT INTERRUPT THE SPEAKER

The patient listener is careful not to interrupt the speaker. We can follow and value the speaker and get so caught up in what she is saying that we might accidentally finish her thought. It might be tempting to see this as a good thing. One might be self-congratulatory, thinking, "I am listening so closely that I can almost read her mind." When we finish her sentence correctly, she might feel listened to, or she might not.

The larger issue occurs when we interrupt and finish the speaker's thought, and we *don't* get it correct. She turned right, and we turned left. Occasionally, someone might be charmed if we finish his or her thoughts correctly. Most of the time, it comes across as saying, "I know you better than you know yourself." However, people are unique in the universe, so this is impossible. More often than not, this action feels disrespectful to the other person. While it might come from good intentions, it is often perceived as being arrogant. Like my mom said when her water heater was broken, "You can't possibly understand what I'm feeling right now."

Following, valuing, and respecting the speaker are the elements of listening patiently.

PATIENT LISTENING CULTIVATES A LIFESTYLE OF PATIENCE

Our ability to listen patiently is connected to a deeper, hidden issue. We are in such a hurry that we don't have time for deep conversations. There are times when it is impossible to engage in patient listening. But, for every one of these moments, there are five other moments when we could listen patiently, and we just don't.

By setting a course toward patient listening, you will find that it increases your patience toward life in general and not just in moments that require your best listening skills.

WHAT KEEPS US FROM LISTENING PATIENTLY?

So what keeps us from becoming patient listeners? I am an adult who has suffered from (or has been blessed with) attention deficit disorder (ADD). My mind races much of the time. When I engage in conversation, I have two sources of distraction with which I must constantly contend: my internal world of hopes, dreams, fears, and worries—*all* that is going on inside my head—and all the stuff going on all around me that is competing for my attention. We call both of these types of distractions *filters*. For the most part, filters make us impatient listeners.

Internal filters are the clutter taking place inside the head: my worries, my thoughts, and my preoccupations.

External filters are what bombard my senses and distract me from any conversation. This is the stuff coming into my head by way of my five senses.

When either internal or external filters are present and competing for our focus on the speaker, we have a formidable barrier that prevents us from being patiently present.

INTERNAL FILTERS

Internal filters are our frame of mind, mood, or emotional state we happen to be in at the moment. For example, when I am really tired, it is difficult for me to listen patiently. I begin to feel impatient and want the speaker to "hurry up and shut up" so I can clear my head. If I am excited about something I'm doing or getting ready to do, I find that it is difficult to remain in the moment and listen patiently to what that person has to say. I want to talk about what *I'm* doing, what *I'm* excited about, what *I'm* struggling with. One of my internal filters is just my world and who I am.

Also, if I have had too much coffee, I get that anxious, jumpy, fidgety feeling, and that pretty much shoots my patience quotient in the foot, and much of what I need to hear is filtered out of the conversation.

A big internal filter for me is unfinished stuff. I haven't gotten my work done, or my projects and to-do lists are getting out of hand. In that case, I have this constant drain on my mental resources. It is as if a part of my mind knows I have stuff to do, and so that part works to keep reminding me of what needs to be done. My brain is actually afraid I'll forget what's important, and so it does what it must to prevent that from happening.

If I keep an up-to-date to-do list, I don't have to spare as many of my brain cells to keep me on track. I carry a little notebook with me all the time. When I think of something that I need to do, I immediately write it down and then later add it to the to-do list on my computer.

This little action provides a *big* reservoir of patience, because I have a lot more mental energy at hand to invest in listening with patience. That stuff needing to be done no longer constantly nags at me to get up and do it. The nagging is my brain's way of not forgetting. I consume a lot of brain energy trying to remember, so if I can use a $2 notebook to increase the RAM in my brain, it's worth every penny because it makes me a much more patient listener.

If, in the course of listening, a distracting "you need to do this" thought zips through my brain, I will stop and say, "There is something I need to jot down on my to-do list. If you will pardon me for just a second while I write it down, I'll be able to give you my undivided attention." Sometimes I don't even explain. I just stop them and say, "Excuse me. I need to write something down." And, after doing so, I face them, relax, and, with my body, I say *I'm ready to listen to you without hurry or interruption.*

Another internal filter is the inflexible agenda. Some of us, like me, don't respond well to the interruptions of life. We have our checklist of tasks we're going to do today, and you'd better *not* get in our way. It always seems like on the days when I have a clear picture of what I need to do, someone crosses my path that needs a very patient listener. Often in those moments I don't want to listen patiently! *Don't you understand my ADD brain needs to go down my to-do list in order to lower my anxiety?*

The listener can't read my mind—which is a good thing—so I have to grapple with my filter and have a talk with myself.

There are chemically-induced internal filters such as drugs, alcohol, and, as we mentioned before, caffeine. While some think that alcohol relaxes you, it does a number on your impulse control. If you are chemically impaired, this simply is not the moment to have that deep conversation, and not observing this creates a whole new area of lifetime regrets.

Finally, there is the end of the day. After having listened and interacted all day, a guy just needs to go inside his cave, put his mind in neutral, and stare at the fire. Since most of us don't have a campfire in our cave, we tend to replicate the flickering sensation by using the controller to switch TV channels. At any rate, we are exhausted, and sometimes we just don't have anything left to provide for others.

If you are tapped out and realize your listening resources are running on empty, just ask your speaker if he or she would give you a rain check on this conversation. Persuade them that you might be more attentive *after* you recharge your battery. You can only do what you can do, so don't try to fake it. Instead, if you're tired, tell the person that you're tired, and if listening right now is a must, he or she will at least understand your momentary shortcomings.

EXTERNAL FILTERS

External filters are the environmental elements that make us impatient listeners. I love music. Chords, harmonies, and the structure of music intrigue me. However, if I'm trying to listen patiently to a person, background music really gets in the way for me. It is like watching TV but having two channels on the same screen at the same time, one superimposed on the other. When the source of distraction is a television or radio, I try to turn it off or move to where I am not distracted by it. Unfortunately I don't always have control over the environment, so I have to work at shutting out the environmental distractions as well as I can.

Once I was presenting a corporate training session in a high-rise building, and there were window washers suspended on a platform outside the classroom. That was quite a distraction! Fortunately they moved on to another floor soon after we began the training session. It would be difficult for me to have a deep conversation at one of those sidewalk cafés in Paris. I would find the passersby way too distracting to keep my focus on the speaker.

To deal with external filters, I try to control where I sit, the background music, and as much of the environment as I can. Then I have to deal with what I can't control by just focusing on the speaker and doing my best to shut everything else out.

HOW DO WE GET THERE?

The way we become a patient listener is by *choosing to be patient.* It is the process of recognizing active, reflective, empathic listening is necessary and then making the choice to switch over to listening patiently. Unfortunately, we don't have a built-in radar or sensor that tells us when someone approaching us needs that kind of listening. Therefore, we become a patient listener by consistently choosing to listen patiently to everyone who speaks to us.

A simple approach might be to start out making one day a week the day in which you attempt to be patient with everyone who speaks to you. I don't enjoy exercising, but I stick with it because I need to. When I miss a day or two, I very quickly drop off my exercise program. I have to steel myself into getting up early. So when I'd rather stay in my warm, comfy bed, I put on my clothes and go exercise. I have to make myself do it.

I discipline myself to do a task that doesn't come naturally for me. The goal in listening is to cultivate a discipline of patience and flexibility that allows you to be in the moment when the moment presents the need to listen. Just like the commercial, it begins by just *doing it.*

WHEN YOU FAIL

Give yourself room to fail. You might be going over your day in your mind and realize that you had a conversation three hours earlier in which you didn't demonstrate much patience.

Don't despair. Listening patiently doesn't come easily for most of us. It's back to that self-centered focus. We are focused on *our* needs and, while it is altruistic and good to listen patiently, we by our very nature tend to default to impatient listening.

It takes time to get to a place where we can catch ourselves in failure, realize just how little the speaker benefits from our impatience, and then resolve to be better next time. This realization empowers us to make the change.

The pain of failure and grieving over that failure motivates us to become successful. It is simply saying, "I didn't listen very patiently this time, but I'm going to do better next time," then following through and doing just that.

Very few of our important conversations are scheduled events. Most happen spontaneously, and we are often caught off guard. We are driving down the road of life headed to Kansas City, and suddenly someone asks us to go with him to Dallas. It takes some work to come to grips with that change. It doesn't feel very good, but in time we become more attuned to others.

After you get better at this, you might begin to catch yourself halfway through the conversation and realize you aren't listening the way you should. Recognizing the need to change in midconversation allows you to simply switch to a patient listening mode. If we continually make the choice to move toward patient listening, we will get there. As with all behaviors we want to change, you must get a mental picture of yourself engaged in that new behavior before you do anything. Just picturing yourself as a patient listener will enable your subconscious mind to move you in that direction.

REPENT!

I am a preacher's kid. I carry around an entire encyclopedia of theological terms in my head. A word I grew up hearing from the pulpit a lot was *repent.* This might summon up all kinds of mental images for you depending on your upbringing, but the word simply means to turn around, make a U-turn, to go back the other way.

If you find you have been driving the wrong way, the best course of action is to stop and make a U-turn. When you find that you are not listening patiently, just repent. Make a U-turn in your head. If you must, tell the speaker, "I'm sorry. I was distracted, and you deserve my undivided attention. Can we start this conversation over again? This time, I want to really *hear* you."

Catching your own interruptions in the moment and making the change right then and there reinforces the desired behavior and tells the speaker you really do want to hear what he or she has to say.

REMAINING PATIENT

When you get to a place where you are listening patiently, how then do you remain there? You might use a term you hear from Dr. Phil—"self talk." You have little conversations with yourself. This act goes a long way to create and sustain patience as a listener. Tell yourself, "Today, I'm going to work hard at being a patient listener" when you are gathering your thoughts in the morning. You will program yourself to do just that.

If you are planning to meet someone for lunch, you can "rehearse" and remind yourself of your determination to listen patiently. Every time you plan ahead this way, you are making that specific neural pathway in your brain a little wider, a little smoother, a little easier to default to your "patience mode" rather than impatience. Over time, you will find that you will listen patiently without even thinking about it. Patient listening is not a skill as much as it is a decision that becomes a habit over time.

CAN'T FAKE IT

When it is impossible for you to listen patiently, just tell the person who is baring their soul to you that you are, for whatever reason, not at your best as a listener at the moment.

Patient listening cannot be faked, and if you try, the speaker will sense your disingenuousness.

When we are impatient, our body language shouts *impatience.* Our posture, the tone of our voice, the movement of our hands, the gaze in our eyes are all dead giveaways that telegraph, "I have better things to do than listen to you."

Don't try to "fake it till you make it." Instead, just be honest about your inability to listen in that moment. Having said this, sometimes just admitting impatience is the very way to enable us to recover and recapture our ability to be patient.

SENSING, PROCESSING, AND RESPONDING: PATIENTLY

Previously, we noted that all types of listening are composed of *sensing, processing,* and *responding.* When we listen patiently, our ability to sense what the person is communicating is heightened. When we are patient, we have a great deal more brainpower to apply to the task of sensing and getting the intended message. One of the benefits of patient listening is it allows you to think. If you're not in a hurry, you can certainly think clearer and process what you hear more effectively. And, if you're not rushed, you have time to think through your responses.

Active, reflective, empathic (ARE) listening *requires* thinking, and the thinking mind is a powerful tool.

Gandhi was able to eject the British out of India because he didn't react impulsively. He was patient. He thought through the process and considered all his options. He waited until he knew what he needed to do, and he waited for the right time to do it. He thought long and hard about what he was going to do until he had a good answer. He accomplished what no army could do, because he was patient.

The serenity that comes with patience allows your brain to process what you hear much more efficiently.

BETTER THINKING = MORE PATIENCE = BETTER THINKING

Because patience improves our ability to think, we are able to move from sensing to processing and carry out the task of decoding and understanding what we are hearing more efficiently. We have the resources to process information quickly and accurately without the distractions that fuel impatience.

I can tell when my computer needs some housecleaning, because functions that normally happen almost instantly begin to take a little longer. I know it's time to take action when I find myself waiting on the machine to think. Unwanted programs are running behind the scenes just burning up computer-processing power and that, combined with all the accumulated spyware and other bad stuff lurking in the background, begins to slow up the process.

So it is with our own brains. It's the background stuff that produces impatience. And, in turn, impatience robs us of our ability to think clearly, and therefore we don't process what we hear. Our response is flawed when we miss this vital component of listening. Thus patience is a huge part of what enables us to sense, process, and respond appropriately.

A DEEPER ISSUE

We learn to listen patiently by choosing to nurture this quality in our character. We maintain patience by self-talk and rehearsing the behavior. It is good to move to a deeper level and think about patience more like a change in lifestyle.

A question to ask ourselves is "*What* are we in a hurry for?" or "*Why* are we always in a hurry?" and "*What* is *more* important than this moment?"

When we do this, we begin to enjoy one of the best benefits of learning to listen deeply and powerfully—we begin to cultivate a patience and flexibility that equips us to deal with the uncertainties of life in a healthier way.

Begin the process by learning to relax when you are caught up in a conversation.

My grandparents owned a plumbing business. My grandmother ran the business until she was nearly eighty years old. In college, I would find myself needing time with her, so I would take off from my studies and head for the shop. She would always spot me the very moment I walked in the door, and she would light up. She would get up from her desk and invite me to join her in a reception area set up like an old-fashioned parlor. She would sit down and take a moment to physically relax and make herself comfortable.

She had a process, a ritual of relaxing before having a conversation. She would grasp a linen handkerchief and twirl it between her fingers like a set of rosary beads, enabling her to expend her own energy while focusing patiently on me. She was a great listener, and she was instinctively aware of her own need to fidget, so she countered that with an activity that allowed her mind to listen patiently.

If you are having trouble relaxing as you work to cultivate a more patient attitude and lifestyle, it is appropriate to determine *why* you are in such a hurry to begin with.

If you are trying to multitask, you need to know that this is one of the great fallacies of time management. Very few people can truly multitask. Most people just do more than one job at the same time poorly and inefficiently. In so doing, we stretch ourselves too thin, which raises our level of anxiety and lowers our level of patience.

Spending a little time in your head and examining what causes impatience pays big dividends in the long run. If you find that you are not able to listen patiently because you're doing too many things, sort out your priorities so that you can make time to listen.

UNDERSTAND YOUR TRIGGERS

I have never met a person who woke up one morning and said, "Today I am going to be especially impatient with those around me." I believe that most of the time, impatience ambushes us. It often starts out as vague feelings that we are not even aware of but, even so, our body knows. It might be a clenching of the jaws, a tightness in our chest or stomach, or just tension in the shoulders.

To deal with impatience, we must be aware of it. So, ask yourself which events, people, phrases, or circumstances seem to wear on your level of patience. Make a list of what causes you anxiety, tension, or frustration. Try to be as thorough as you can.

You will most likely find that most triggers are rooted in an underlying belief that we don't want to face. For example, the impatience we feel is because at the very core of our belief system lays the notion that when a person comes to us with a problem, we must fix it. However, most issues that people bring to us are way beyond our ability to fix.

If our value system is guided by the mandate that we *must* fix people, and we know we can't, we have an impossible conflict, and we pull away from the impossible. Facing that I have this need to fix people and understanding that this is impossible spells R-E-L-I-E-F! Accepting this impossibility is liberating. I no longer feel compelled to "do something," and understanding this releases me to just listen, patiently.

AFTER DISCOVERING YOUR TRIGGERS

Just let go of stuff. At times, something will block you from listening patiently, and you won't be able to do anything about it. Just recognize it, understand what it is, and then just let it go. Practice makes perfect, so practice this: the next time you're waiting in line in a store and you feel impatient, stop, let it go, and notice how it will free you up to relate to those around you in a new and relaxed way. You'll find yourself engaging with people and truly hearing them and feeling unhurried and thankful for the opportunity that came from a long wait in a checkout lane at the grocery store.

THE BOTTOM LINE

Learning to listen patiently is just making a choice, and mindfully and consistently repeating that choice makes it second nature. However, cultivate an attitude of patience toward life in general. It is essential in taking the first step to becoming a powerful listener.

In the beginning of this chapter, I spoke about my son calling at an inconvenient time. That phone call was really a wake-up call for me and a reminder of the importance of my role as a father to listen to my sons. That *is* who I want to be. I was struck by the realization that of all I could aspire to in life, being a dad who patiently listens to his sons should be right at the very top of the list. After I'm dead and gone, I want my sons to remember me as a father who always had time to listen, patiently.

ACTIVITIES: PRACTICE, PONDER, PENCIL, PLOT, AND PREPARE

1. **Practice** patience:
   Monitor your listening this week.
   Focus on listening patiently this week.
   Notice what happens when someone needs to talk to you at a very inopportune time.
   Daily: Schedule a few minutes before every meeting on your calendar to prepare yourself by "rehearsing to listen patiently."

2. **Ponder:**
   Think of someone in your life that you really liked and felt drawn to and who enjoyed being with you. Picture this person in your mind. Recall a memory where you spent time with that person. What quality made him or her so fun to be around? Was listening patiently part of that?

3. **Pencil:**
   Journal. Get a small notebook. Keep track of your conversation. Rate your conversations on a scale of one to five, with five being very patient. After you have a conversation, evaluate your level of patience. When you get that irritated, fidgety feeling or find yourself distracted in conversation, make a note of that. Note the conversation and why you think you might have been impatient. Example: *Conversation with Bill Smith on Thursday. I was impatient; I was worried that I would be late for the meeting.* Tracking and evaluating the quality of your listening abilities in your conversations will make you improve. Someone once said, "Nothing gets done that doesn't get measured." By measuring your performance, you will improve your performance.

4. **Plot Your Path:**
   Track and Analyze Impatient Moments
   In your journal, make note of those times when you feel impatient. It might not feel like full-blown impatience, so be sensitive to feeling rushed or just fidgety and anxious. Impatience might present itself as just distraction and an inability to focus. Whatever you experience that "filters" or blocks you from being there in the moment with the speaker is something you need to write down. Now try to pinpoint what that feeling is associated with. It is important that you consistently and consecutively record each

time the feeling occurs. This will make you more aware of the feeling of impatience. Journaling this will enable you to observe the sense of impatience objectively and discover the events that precipitate your impatience. Some people discover after journaling that it is not necessarily an event that is causing impatience but the feeling itself. By documenting the process, you will be able to control your impatience when it interferes with your listening abilities.

5. **Prepare for Relapses:**
   Controlling Impatience. We all have relapses. To err is human, remember? You can, however, make changes when you find yourself listening impatiently by learning to relax in that moment. The key is to take a few deep breaths and then try to clear your mind. If that doesn't work, just focus on the act of breathing. Notice your inhaling and exhaling, and let the rhythm and cycle of your breathing be a calming factor.

Chapter Seven

LISTEN WITH YOUR BODY

"The average person looks without seeing
listens without hearing
touches without feeling
moves without physical awareness
and talks without thinking."
Leonardo Da Vinci

He looked directly into the camera and said he wanted to address the American people. He gripped the podium with one hand and waved the other like a loaded gun, using it to drive home his point even before he said those famous words: *"I did not have sexual relations with that woman, Miss Lewinski."* He punctuated each word with emphasis, shaking his head side to side as he spoke. He said all the right phrases and used all the right gestures, but the American people didn't believe him. Eventually, he came clean and admitted his wrongdoing.

In this short video clip of President Clinton's press conference, he is polished and rehearsed, but his performance just doesn't come across as credible. What did he do or say that gave him away? What specific word or phrase actually betrayed his veracity? Something just didn't ring true.

Later on, he was called to testify before a grand jury about his relationship with Monica Lewinski. This same Bill Clinton used a neutral style of body language when he was responding truthfully to questions. However, as the questions became more specific and focused more on his behavior with Lewinski, he frequently touched his nose.

This underscores the theory that when we tell a lie, our body is so programmed to tell the truth that we instinctively reach up to cover our mouth. A sophisticated liar will instead touch his nose. Either way, nose or mouth, the impulse to be truthful is so deeply embedded in our subconscious mind that even when we attempt to lie, our body just can't seem to go along with the ruse.

Body language will betray even the most skillful of liars, because our body is wired to simply tell the truth. The science of nonverbal communication describes this as the incongruence of words and the body.

Our body language as a listener can either enhance or detract from our own responses to the speaker. Our words and actions must line up for our responses to be genuine. The response doesn't ring true when it and the accompanying body language don't match up.

To be a great listener, it is important to clearly understand *how* one responds with his or her body speaks far more clearly than anything he or she can say with words. The listener's body language will either convey "I'm listening to you" or "I would rather be somewhere else."

As a powerful listener, you must find a way to listen to the speaker's body language and, at the same time, respond sincerely with your own body.

IN THE BEGINNING

While formal research on nonverbal communication began in the mid-1900s, there have always been astute observers of body language.

Sigmund Freud noticed, while one of his patients talked about how happy she was in her marriage, she was sliding her wedding ring on and off her finger.

In 1950, the original researcher on nonverbal communication or "kinesics" observed the average person speaks ten to eleven minutes a day, and the average sentence takes 2.5 seconds to complete. The researcher, Ray Birdwhistell, discovered there was more body language, or nonverbal communication, going on than had ever been documented. He noted we can recognize more than 250,000 facial expressions. So, for all the words we say in our ten minutes, we have an extensive repertoire of body movements and postures to reinforce those words.

In 1971, UCLA researcher Albert Mehrabian found only 7 percent of our communication actually comes from our words. Also, 38 percent of our communication comes from the nonverbal part of our speech—the inflection, tone, pitch, and pace of our words.

Moreover, Mehrabian observed 55 percent of our communication comes from our body language. This means that 93 percent of our communication is inflection and nonverbal.

This research begs the questions: do we really understand what a person is saying to us? Do we really know how to understand the language of the body? Are you just listening to that person's words, or are you attending to the other 93 percent of what they are saying with their body language?

One of the three components of listening is *sensing*, the process of gathering accurate data. Not attending to body language will have an enormous impact on the quality and accuracy of the information we are sensing. Our perception will be impaired, resulting in faulty processing, a poor response, and ineffective communication without a clear understanding of body language.

TRUST THE BODY OVER THE VOICE

In recent years, researchers have discovered when a discrepancy exists between the message in the words and the message communicated by the body, human beings will choose the veracity of body language over words.

A recent research project used photographs of fearful, angry, and happy faces and bodies, with either matched or mismatched emotional expressions. The researchers found the observer tends to be biased toward the emotions expressed by the body when the face and body convey conflicting emotional expressions. When there is a contradiction between the body and the voice, the body trumps voice every time.

Initially, we are more likely to believe what we see over what we hear. There is a biological explanation for this. The way the brain stores perceived information lends itself to a bias of the visual over the auditory. Therefore, it is incumbent on us to look for messages in the speaker's body language.

The reason why the body carries a lot more weight over words is the body is a lot more truthful. We can easily mislead or just downright lie with our voice, but the unconscious is compelled to speak truthfully through the body. It is as if the body is so programmed to tell the truth that *even* in a lie, the body tries to tell the truth. In a lie, the body will give cues that betray the deception, because your body always expresses your true feelings.

If you are bored, your body will say so. If you are engaged in the conversation, your body will communicate "engaged." Those around you are constantly reading your body language, whether you like it or not. You'll be nailed every time if your words say one thing and your body says something contradictory. Our bodies can't very easily fake the truth when attempting to deceive, but we *can* enhance our words when speaking the truth by using body language that conforms with and affirms our words.

LISTEN WITH YOUR BODY: A TWO-WAY STREET

A two-way street exists. Our body language assures the listener we got the message and, at the same time, we must accurately sense and interpret the body language of the speaker. Not an easy task!

LISTENING WITH MY BODY

The most important message the listener's body language needs to communicate is safety, ease, and a sense of being comfortable. Skillful listening requires responding, and the listener will either communicate relaxation and comfort or anxiety.

In active, reflective, empathic listening, we want our response to clearly say, "*I am open and receptive to what you have to say.*" We will either speak with open body language or closed body language. Anticipate those important conversations and, as with listening patiently, rehearse listening with your body. Picture beforehand *how* you want to present your posture, so that when you get caught up in the conversation, you have already programmed your body to respond appropriately to the speaker.

MIRRORING GESTURES

A simple place to begin listening with your body is to mirror the speaker's gestures. Mirroring means that you are matching similar gestures and posture and reflecting those actions back to the speaker. It doesn't mean that you are mimicking her or becoming her shadow. Instead, by merely adopting similar movements, you increase the level of rapport and raise the comfort level for the speaker.

Research indicates mirroring builds rapport because it provides a sense of familiarity. The brain registers similar movements in others and sends the message "This person is like me. I can trust them."

Researchers Rizzolatte and Gallese from the University of Parma discovered a unique type of cell called *mirror neurons.* These neurons affect muscle and body movements, and they fire a signal in the brain when we observe what another person experiences or is about to experience.

Mirror neurons enable us to feel what we perceive others are experiencing. We duck if we witness someone taking a swing at another person's face. These cells enable us to see and empathize with others, because our mirror neurons reflect what we observe. Someone laughs, and we end up laughing too. If you're in a dance club and a fast, exciting song begins to play, you'll undoubtedly notice that people will begin to move to the music. Yawn, and the whole world will yawn with you. Smile and…you get the picture.

These neurons enable us to follow other's actions and get in tune with their movements. Their existence appears to be an indication that we are hardwired by nature to be empathetic. Get in touch with them by allowing your body to feel what the speaker is telling you. Wince if it hurts. Laugh if it's amusing.

The greatest obstacle to hearing what our mirror neurons are telling us is just not allowing our body to feel what we should feel when we are listening to others.

Get interested in people. Give yourself permission to empathize with them, and let the body react. Allow this to occur naturally. It builds a connection between the speaker and the listener, and it also builds a deeper level of trust and familiarity.

In a research project on mirror neurons, a group of 120 participants were shown pictures of various facial expressions. The observers noticed a significant number of involuntary responses in facial expressions, and the subjects couldn't restrain the involuntary muscle movement, mirroring what they observed.

We have to work hard at *not* mirroring. Emergency response workers go to great efforts to shut out this involuntary response to their own mirror neurons so that they can get the job done without over-empathizing with victims in emergency situations. Mirror behavior can be seen in animals as well. I have two Jack Russell terriers. When I am trying to prompt one of them to "speak," or bark, in order to receive a treat, the other one will involuntarily "speak." He just can't contain himself, and his mirror neurons are getting the best of him.

I don't enjoy watching slapstick comedy, because I mirror too much. When I was a child, my mother enjoyed an early TV show called *I Love Lucy*. The main character, Lucy, was constantly getting into tight spots, which always spelled trouble with Ricky, her husband.

I suspect because of my own history as a high-spirited child, I related to her shame at being caught in an uncomfortable predicament. Ricky would often come home from work, only to find her in some silly or embarrassing situation. His line was always "Lucy, you got some 'splainin' to do."

My mirror neurons anticipated Lucy's chagrin, which was unbearably unpleasant for me to watch. It was just too close to home, and my mirror cells did their job very well.

Our mirror neurons provide part of what we need to relate to others, and the essence of good listening is exactly that, relating to the speaker. Our goal is to empathize with him or, simply put, "walk in his shoes." In doing this, we are feeling what he feels. This enhances our ability to sense, perceive, and respond to him.

Part of our humanity is that we have the ability to be attuned to what others experience, and when we allow ourselves to honor that humanness, we become better listeners in the process. Mirror neurons make this possible.

LEANING TOWARD THEM

Begin to practice listening with your body. One easy-to-remember step is to simply lean toward the speaker. People who like each other or feel comfortable with each other tend to lean toward each other.

Leaning is like sharing space with the other person. It sends the message "I want to be close to you. I feel comfortable and safe around you," and it encourages the speaker to feel the same way. This is a tool interviewers use to make the person they are interviewing feel relaxed and comfortable.

People open up when they feel secure, and they close up when they don't. When this happens, communication comes to a standstill.

EYE CONTACT

In healthy conversations, the listener makes eye contact 70 to 80 percent of the time according to researcher Michael Argyle. If you are shy or introverted and feel uncomfortable looking people in the eye, this is an issue that you can—and need—to overcome with time and practice. Just like the rest of the body, the eyes don't lie. They either say "I'm comfortable and interested in what you have to say" or "I would rather be somewhere—anywhere—else but here with you."

If you establish a triangle between the eyes and mouth, you have created the *social gaze triangle*. This is the facial zone where people are comfortable gazing at and being gazed at in social situations. It is nonthreatening and creates a sense of connection when done well. You can build good rapport if you maintain good eye contact 60 to 80 percent of the time you are listening to the speaker. Good eye contact is the easiest way to communicate "I'm really listening to you."

Distinguish between good eye contact and a serial-killer stare, which is unwavering, unchanging, and often devoid of blinking. Most of us blink about fifteen times per minute. When we blink less than this, we begin to appear to stare, even when we aren't. If you drop down to four to five times per minute, you will appear to be bored at best and staring at worst.

Break your gaze by looking away just a little. Make sure you aren't looking far from their face as you break the gaze, or they will get the impression you're looking at the clock.

Since I suffer from attention deficit disorder (ADD), I am so distractible that when I'm having a conversation that draws on powerful listening, I intentionally position myself where I won't see people entering or leaving, or TV shows in the background, or anything that would rob me of my ability to concentrate.

Practice by standing in front of a mirror. Turn away from the mirror for a moment. Widen your eyes as if you are really interested in something being said. Notice the facial sensations you felt as you created that expression. Now turn and replicate that sensation in front of the mirror. Observe your eyes. Did you express with your eyes what you set out to express, or did your face say something you didn't intend? Now create the expression you intended to create while looking in the mirror.

Learn to recognize what this feels like, and now be mindful of using your eyes and facial expressions to say, "That's interesting." Then, practice until you can recognize and activate this expression without having to look in the mirror.

CAUTION: CULTURAL DIFFERENCES

Some Asian and Native American cultures perceive direct eye contact as threatening, rude, or disrespectful. Observe the level of eye contact between you and persons from another culture and try to match that until you know them better. Do some research on the spot if you find yourself in a deep conversation with an Asian. Tell him or her that you understand that some cultures are uncomfortable with eye contact and ask him or her how he or she feels about this.

Your goal is to listen in a way that allows the speaker to truly feel heard. You certainly want to know about it if something helps him or her feel more comfortable. Become aware of what your eyes are telling the speaker. Are you "reflecting" or responding with your eyes? Do your eyes reflect the emotion the speaker is feeling or describing? Be aware of your eyes and facial expressions as you listen.

THOU SHALL NOT

Generally, in listening, don't look from side to side. Don't look down at the speaker's body. Don't even try to sneak a downward look. Your peripheral vision is not *that* good, and the speaker *will* notice. My wife tells me this is especially true for females. They tend to be particularly keen on catching misplaced glances. If you do, you'll go from being a good listener to letch, and it is very difficult to recover from this little blunder.

Don't peer over reading glasses when listening, unless you want to plant the image of the stern schoolteacher or defense attorney in the speaker's mind. Take them off to listen to the speaker, and please take off your sunglasses when listening, even outside. There's a reason why professional poker players wear sunglasses. They know the eyes are a dead giveaway to our thoughts, so they cover them up. Unless you're at the poker table in Vegas, don't hide your eyes behind anything.

FACIAL EXPRESSION

What do your facial expressions tell the speaker? Learn to be at ease. Your goal is to be "in the moment," to make this the most important action you are or could be doing. Learn to relax that face. Develop a ritual of consciously relaxing your face while listening. Be mindful that sometimes tension settles in our jaws, eyes, eyebrows, or forehead.

Develop your own routine to intentionally release tension, and let it go. Replace it with a smile. Remember, a little smile builds a lot of rapport. A smile says, "I'm not going to hurt you. You're safe!"

Smiles have a physiological effect on our system by releasing neurotransmitters that increase our sense of security and well-being. Learn to smile as you listen to people speak. Of course, if they're telling you that their mother died, you don't necessarily want to smile in response to that.

Much of the time in conversations, we drift into a deep level of concentration, our faces sag, and we begin to look somber and stern. Remember our goal is to make the speaker comfortable, and stern doesn't cut it.

IS IT A REALLY-MEAN-IT SMILE?

Ever notice someone trying to smile when his or her heart is really not in it? Your face will betray you if you are faking a smile or smiling when you don't feel like smiling.

There is actually a science to this.

Researchers Ekman and Freisen developed an evaluation called the Facial Action Coding System. This evaluation is based on the hypothesis that a real smile is a product of the unconscious and cannot be faked. A genuine smile is a reaction to something and, with the real deal, we are reacting to emotions—both ours and the emotions of those around us. In a genuine smile, our mouth changes shape, our cheeks rise, our eyes crinkle up, and our eyebrows dip ever so slightly.

These characteristics can be "faked" with practice, but most feigned smiles merely involve a change in the shape of the lips. The observer's brain might not consciously know what the difference is. However, they will on some subconscious level certainly be aware of the discrepancy in a disingenuous smile.

The best course of action is to just learn to delight in people so, when you smile, you are doing it from the heart and not just the head. A real smile is *always* real. Besides, a smile is contagious. You might find yourself smiling and catch a smile reflected back to you and get infected, with joy.

ARE YOU AWARE OF THE SMIRK?

President George Bush was ever so maligned for his uneven smile. It was often interpreted as a smirk. And, a smirk communicates "I don't trust you." Look at yourself in the mirror. Do you smirk, and, if so, can you change?

Along with the smirky looking smiler is the lip biter. You may be nervous or just have a habit of doing this, but don't. Biting your lips makes you appear to be untrustworthy.

My father-in-law was a brilliant, introspective man. You could always tell when he was deep in thought, because he would grimace. If you saw him for the first time while he was in a reflective moment, you would probably get the impression he was mad at the world because, when pondering over the meaning of life, he appeared to be quite dour.

Be aware of what you do and the faces you make when you're not thinking about *how* you look.

USING YOUR HEAD LANGUAGE?

Our Jack Russell terriers love ice. The dogs congregate at my feet when I serve myself ice from the door dispenser on the refrigerator. As the ice is crushed and slips down the chute into my glass, they look up, tilting their heads in tandem as if to say, "Fascinating how ice comes out of that big white box." When your dog is curious, he or she will tilt his or her head to the right. Learn a great trick from them.

When listening intently, tilt your head slightly to the right, and you will be saying, "I'm interested. Tell me more." This action is a sign of vulnerability. You're saying, "I trust you enough to set aside caution and safety to really hear what you're saying." Raise your eyebrows, and you reinforce the message. And finally, don't ever turn your head to one side as if to shut the other person out.

If you blunder and unintentionally say or do something with your actions, just have a conversation about it with the other person and go on with your listening.

ARE YOU NODDING?

Nodding is another way to show agreement to confirm you're following the conversation and don't want to interrupt the speaker. Remember, listening is about perceiving, processing, and responding. The nod is one very simple way to respond to the speaker, and research indicates nodding is a very unobtrusive way to encourage the speaker to continue. It also clearly shows understanding.

A slow, deliberate nod says, "I see your point." Speed up your nodding just a little, and you will demonstrate that you see the bigger picture. Just remember that nodding too fast says, "I get the picture already, so shut up."

Note that a nodding response does not necessarily say, "I agree with you." Instead, it affirms the message, "I hear you. Tell me more."

HOW ABOUT YOUR HANDS?

The open palm clearly communicates, "I am open to what you are saying." When listening, let your hands hang at your sides when standing and open and relaxed in your lap when seated.

Clenched fists or folded hands take away from communicating openness and receptiveness. They will instead communicate frustration, hostility, and a negative attitude. Gesture using palms facing upward and open when reflecting back what you have heard the speaker say. This is a universal symbol for openness that even chimpanzees use when they practice good listening.

When speaking, don't point. Think of a pointed hand gesture as a loaded gun, and use it only for self-defense. Powerful listening should *never* be a defensive endeavor, so leave your guns at home. Press your index finger against your thumb as if you are holding something if you *must* use it to make a point. You will still have the power of a pointed finger without making a threatening gesture.

Use the thumbs-up sign to communicate approval. I recently read a motivational book by Francis X. Maguire entitled *You're the Greatest!* The picture on the front cover is of the author with his thumb up. The point of the book is appreciating others. Without overdoing it, a simple thumbs-up for others is a great way of communicating approval.

CROSSED ARMS?

Crossing our arms makes us feel safe when we are feeling exposed. It warms us when we feel cold, but it also clearly says: *I am defensive. I am protecting myself. I am not open to what you want to say.* Crossed arms shout, "The door to my mind is closed, locked, and bolted." Never cross your arms if you are trying to listen with your body. It doesn't just give the illusion of not listening, you actually *don't* absorb as much if you're listening with your arms crossed.

Research indicates when people listen with their arms crossed they learn 38 percent less than those who listen with open arms. That same study revealed when people listen with their arms crossed, they have a higher percentage of negative thoughts about the speaker. All this underscores the tremendous connection between body and mind when it comes to powerful listening.

ARE YOU TOUCHING?

Are you the touchy-feely person who *must* reach out and touch another person? If so, touch their elbow. Research from the University of Minnesota finds that gently touching a person on the elbow creates a momentary bond. The elbow is the one "safe," nonthreatening place to touch, and when conversing this type of touch creates a predisposition for rapport and cooperation.

THE LANGUAGE OF BODY STILLNESS

Learn not to fidget, play with your fingers, twirl your hair, stroke your beard, or twitch while listening. My grandmother was able to expend her nervous energy during listening by playing with a hanky. But most people can't pull this off. Settling your body down is the art of *active* listening in a *passive* fashion. Body movement telegraphs distracting thoughts and feelings.

On the other hand, stillness is not just an act. It actually enables you to forget everything else except the other person. Rather than acting, it is actually the process of becoming still that places you firmly in the moment where even your own thoughts are not allowed to distract you from the speaker.

WHAT'S YOUR ANGLE?

The angle at which you position yourself speaks volumes. Sit at a forty-five-degree angle to the person, and you will communicate comfortable, cooperative, and congenial. Note that a ten-degree shift either way communicates something different: ten degrees more toward the speaker says deeper intimacy is possible; ten degrees less says "I want to shut you out."

Whether standing or sitting, positioning yourself at a forty-five- degree angle from the speaker seems to be most conducive to great conversations. Try not to face the speaker straight on, as this is a defensive posture both humans and animals take when preparing for confrontation. Try not to turn your shoulders away from the speaker, as this communicates "I'm not comfortable with you."

Relax, especially your shoulders and upper body. Breathe deeply and allow your chest to open. Relax those arms. The same goes for legs. Relax your body and uncross anything that might be crossed.

ARE YOU STANDING?

Position yourself at a forty-five-degree angle to the speaker's right if you're having a conversation while standing. Don't stand straight face to face or head on with the speaker. When animals prepare to fight, they face each other head on. As with animals, people feel most comfortable when conversing at a forty-five-degree angle.

Stand at a comfortable distance, arms open and hands visible, with a welcoming expression on your face. Stand side by side at the appropriate distance, and you will communicate connection. Don't stand frozen and still in place. Move a little without being fidgety. Don't rock back and forth, and don't tap your feet or keep a rhythm.

Stand with your legs hip-width apart. Evenly distribute your weight on each leg. Don't stand with your legs far apart like the guys at the OK Corral just before they drew their guns. If you do, this is the image the speaker will get, and you can expect defensiveness on his part.

Don't stand with your legs crossed. It looks like you need to empty your bladder, and don't stand with one leg turned to a forty-five-degree angle. It looks like you're trying to dart out the door at the first indication the coast is clear. Shift your body a little from time to time. And, finally, remember what your mom told you: "Stand up straight!"

HOW ABOUT THOSE FEET?

Feet flat on the floor, pointed toward the speaker, say "I am listening and I am trustworthy." As you monitor your body for good listening habits, remember we are least aware of our outer extremities. Since our feet are farthest from our brain, we are the most unaware of what they are saying when we are listening. The good news is that they are pretty honest about the person's feelings. Also, the bad news is that they are pretty honest about the person's feelings.

Are your legs crossed? Are your feet pointed toward the door? Are you tapping your foot? Do you have fidgety feet? One of the primary reasons we have feet is to get us away from danger so, when we feel uncomfortable or threatened, it will be apparent in our legs and feet.

Beware: if you are feeling impatient or wanting to get out of the conversation, you will probably find that your feet are pointed toward your exit route. Our body is just *that* honest, and there is no hiding what we really want.

HOW CLOSE IS TOO CLOSE?

Researcher Edward Hall coined the term *proxemics*, which is the science of how conversations are affected by the distance between two individuals during interaction. He determined there are comfort zones of proximity that correspond to the appropriate level of intimacy in a given situation. Each zone has a range and comfort level, which varies depending primarily on where you're from.

The level of comfortable closeness varies for different cultures. People from densely populated areas are much more comfortable with physical close proximity during a conversation than ranchers from Montana are. Also, be aware if you are moving too close to someone in conversation, his or her body language will let you know. Start at what Hall calls the "social zone," about four feet from the speaker. Too close, and you'll come across as too familiar. Too distant, and you'll be perceived as rude or standoffish.

While the social zone for listeners is anywhere from four to twelve feet, it is best to work the four-foot area as your target. If people draw you in, move toward them. The comfort of closeness varies from culture to culture. The Japanese, who live in tight proximity, are more comfortable being close up and personal.

Authors Alan and Barbara Pease describe "The Japanese/ American waltz." A Japanese businessman will move close when conversing with his American counterpart. The American, unaccustomed to that level of closeness, will take a step backward. This precipitates more forward movement by the Japanese person, followed by another step backward by the American. The authors conclude that if you made a video of the interaction and increased the playback speed, the people would appear to be waltzing.

Consider the comfort level of the other person in the interaction. This requires sensitivity and observation. As the conversation progresses, move closer to the other person. Watch for cues that betray discomfort and, if you reach that point, simply take a step backward. When you get too close, you will cause a physiological reaction. The speaker's heart rate and blood pressure will go up, and anxiety levels will also rise.

Watch for stepping back, averting a gaze, a sudden stop in conversation, and body language that would appear defensive or closing. If you suspect you've violated space, take a step or two back.

We want people to move toward being comfortable and open instead of closed and anxious. We do that by sending messages with our body that say loudly and clearly, "You are safe with me. I am open and not a threat to you, and I am really interested in what you say." You will be successful at listening by relaxing your body and being fascinated with what the speaker is saying.

You will gradually improve these skills without needing a checklist if you practice relaxing with your body every time you have a conversation, even a phone conversation.

Powerful listening—or as we have called it, ARE (active, reflective, empathic) listening—begins by sincerely listening calmly and patiently with your body. The source of information that comes from observing the speaker's body is the most reliable. If you learn to focus on people and see them as unique and precious with priceless stories to tell, your body will truthfully reflect that belief. Remember, our words and actions must match.

WHEN YOU'VE LOST IT

There are times when listening fatigue or just being generally tired gets the best of us. Just apologize for the distraction when this happens. Make a mental commitment to resume good listening and recover a body attitude of openness.

You can do this by taking a deep breath. Get some oxygen in your system without letting out a big sigh. Gently open your chest as if you're showing off something really important. Tilt your head a little to the right, focus on the words you're hearing, use your breathing to get centered back on the speaker, and return to being in the moment. Smile, keep blinking, nod, and shift your body a little to wake yourself up and commit to doing better next time.

LISTENING TO THE SPEAKER'S BODY

You must also become fluent in understanding the body language that is coming *from* the speaker. Otherwise, the amount of sensing that takes place will be severely limited to a small fraction of the actual content. It is difficult to process a picture when you are missing 93 percent of the information.

Once we have accurately sensed and processed the information, we must be able to respond appropriately. This requires that we develop a level of fluency in reading the speaker's body message and communicating, "I'm hearing what you said, and I understand" without having to resort to words.

Researcher Albert Mehrabian found the message the speaker is sending us is primarily based on how they appear or, in other words, what does their body language say? How do they sound? What are the inflections in their voice? And least of all, *what are they saying?*

Apply this to powerful ARE listening, and the process of learning to listen to what the speaker is communicating with his or her body is one of the most important tools we can use to become a great listener.

You're missing a lot of your program if 55 percent of your TV screen is blank. If that percent is too dark or washed out, you're not going to be very satisfied with the quality of the program. Contrast that with a TV screen where the entire picture is clear, vibrant, and full of rich details. This is the difference learning to listen to the others' body language makes. Listen to their body language. You will get the full picture, in color!

As you listen, it is helpful to observe what signals the speakers' bodies are sending. Are they looking off and away or down at the floor? Is their body closed—arms crossed and fists clenched? Their body is an indicator of their comfort level. Does it read "anxious" or "comfortable?"

As the listener, it is your job to notice these cues and do what you can to increase their comfort and security and set the stage for them to open up and be heard.

If their body is a picture, could you describe that picture back to them? You might see discomfort in their body and respond by saying, "You seem really uncomfortable with this conversation," or "You really don't take much pleasure in talking about this, do you?" Accurately read and reflect back the body language they are presenting. You will be able to make an appropriate response, and you will open the door for them to grapple with their feelings. More often than not, an accurate reflective response like this will actually lead to openness on the speaker's part rather than increased defensiveness.

EITHER, OR

So how do we become proficient in reading body language? Start by remembering that all body language is saying either, "I'm comfortable and at ease" or "I'm anxious and wary."

You will be well on your way to understanding body language when you become skilled at reading these two categories, but these are general. Be cautious. Remember the old saying "one swallow doesn't make a spring." Body language is equivalent to words, and words must be arranged into sentences before they take on meaning.

CLUSTERS, CONGRUENCE, AND CONTEXT

In reading body language, you don't just take one element and derive a conclusion on the basis of that one action. You look for *clusters*. For example, how the person holds his hands is one action. Besides holding his hands, is he crossing his arms? Avoiding eye contact? All at once? If so, he is exhibiting a *cluster* of actions.

The objective is to look for clusters or combinations of body language. From this we can construe meaning.

Think of this in terms of composition. Sentences are made of words. As with an isolated word out of context, one single action alone doesn't convey much meaning. That same word used in a short sentence suddenly carries powerful impact and meaning.

Actions are like words, and clusters of actions become the sentences that tell you something about the emotional state of the speaker. You don't really have meaning until the words are arranged into sentences.

Also you need to look for *congruence*. Words and body language match when they are *congruent*. Someone tells you she really loves her job, but she is frowning, fidgeting, and showing general discomfort. The message is incongruent, and we are more likely to *not* believe the speaker's verbal message.

The third element to consider is *context*. You are listening to someone. His arms and legs are crossed, his head is down, and he's not making eye contact. With this information alone, you might conclude that he is guarded and not being forthright. However, the context is he is homeless, sitting outdoors at a bus stop. The temperature is twenty-two degrees. Context tells you that there is more to the story than being closed. It says he is just plain cold.

WHAT *NOT* TO DO

You must become a consummate observer of people and cultivate an awareness of the subconscious elements that compel the body to speak the truth at all times.

Begin to observe people in public places as they relate to each other. You will—without hearing the words—quickly pick up on the nuances of what people say with their bodies.

In sales, the body language of a reluctant customer will come through loud and clear. So, if you can spot that resistance in their body language, you can then address their misgivings immediately without giving them time to fester and grow. Often, just recognizing the emotion and reflecting it back to the person enables him to grapple with those feelings and move to a more receptive place.

One of the secrets of successful salespeople is listening for the prospective customer's pain. Buyers make purchases because they want something to be different. They want to feel good. Salespeople find pain drives the buyer and, when encouraged to talk about that pain, they provide the information needed to make the sale. Look for body language that displays discomfort, and it will lead you to their pain. Listen to their pain, and they will be ready to buy.

IMPLICATIONS

The science of body language and communication is still in its infancy. There is much yet to be discovered. The mind-body connection in listening is far more complex than we can imagine. Our bodies will communicate openness and interest when we focus intently on the speaker. Our receptivity and interest is increased when we open our bodies. It brings us back to the old question, "Which came first, the chicken or the egg?"

Listening with fascination for others makes us listen better with our bodies. Mindfully use your body to listen. You will actually understand and retain more.

WHAT'S IN IT FOR ME?

As we listen well, with our bodies, we will become more re-laxed and more comfortable around people. We will also re-member more. As we previously mentioned, research indicates people listening with an open-body posture, such as arm and legs not crossed, actually retain more of what they heard than control groups who listened with closed body language.

Listening with your body will enable you to remember more, and you will become more other-centered and comfortable in your own skin. Increasing your awareness of others around you is a straightforward way of moving from self-centeredness, at worst, or ignorance, at best, to being aware of the needs and internal worlds of others.

You can't reach out to people if you're not even aware they have needs. The benefit of listening with your body is it impacts you as a person. Somehow, listening with our body makes us more human in the best sense of the word.

ACTIVITIES: RESEARCH AND REFLECT

1. Take a trip to your local mall and just sit in the food court area and watch people in conversa-tion. Without being able to hear their words, try to determine the emotional tone of the conver-sation. Look at what message their bodies are sending. Set aside fifteen minutes a day to watch people's body language—anywhere people in-teract. As you observe, you will come to under-stand your own body language better.

2. Turn on the TV. Find a sitcom or drama. Turn the volume down, and just watch the body language. Focus on what they are saying with their bodies.

3. Think of others who "listen" well with their bodies. Imitate them. Think about what it is exactly they do with their bodies that communicates openness. Consider the message that person sends.

4. Start a conversation with someone you know. As he or she speaks, nod your head in encouragement. See what effect your head movements have. Then, stop nodding and see what happens. Communicate attentiveness. Widen your eyes.

5. Stand in front of a full-length mirror.
   a. Observe your head, facial expressions, stance, and posture. What are you communicating?
   b. Turn away. Decide how you want to be perceived.
   c. Pose in that body language and turn back toward the mirror. What similarities and differences do you notice from the first and second postures?

Read More:
The Power of Body Language by Tonya Reiman, Pocket Books/Simon & Schuster, 2007
The Definitive Book of Body Language by Allan and Barbara Pease, Bantam, 2006

Chapter Eight

LISTEN WITH YOUR VOICE

"A powerful agent is the right word.
When we come upon one of those intensely right words
the resulting effect is physical as well as spiritual,
and electrically prompt."
Mark Twain

The client tried to contain his anxiety as he sat nervously in the attorney's office. To most of us, the legal world is an altogether different universe with its own language, liturgy, customs, and unspoken rules. The attorney was asking a lot of questions and writing volumes on a legal pad. There was a structure to the interview. The attorney asked questions that helped him get the chronology of the story, quietly jotting down details that would help him represent his client.

In his world, he was just doing his job. He was *sensing*, gathering information, and *processing* information by shaping it into a narrative he would use to prevail in court.

However, his client was in a very different state of mind.

Being unfamiliar with the legal system, he didn't know what all the words meant, nor did he understand *what* and *why* a particular issue was important. Since all of this was alien to him, he simply didn't know what the attorney needed. And so it just seemed like a series of random questions.

The attorney continued to ask question after question without ever looking up from his own notes. The client fearfully tried to recall every little detail. He was terrified he would leave out the *one* point that would make his case. His anxiety ramped up as the session wound down.

Was his counsel getting all the pertinent facts? Was he hearing what he needed? Was he really listening? The attorney was, after all, writing nonstop. He was in continuous motion, never having finished writing before asking the next question. He was unrelenting, and the uncertainty of it all made the client worry even more. What if the attorney didn't get all the facts, and they lost the case because of this? The client was stressed by the fear that he might have missed something.

Months later at the trial, the client was relieved to hear his lawyer plead his case successfully. He marveled at the incredible details he heard from his attorney's mouth. It was as if the attorney not only heard every word he had told him, but he also captured his very feelings and thoughts in the matter.

At the end of a successful trial, the client's only regret was that if he had somehow known how well the attorney had "heard" him in the beginning, he would have been a lot less anxious and a lot more confident in the days and weeks leading up to the trial.

The attorney was practiced at the first two components of good listening. He *sensed*—or heard—the client's words and perceived the many messages embedded within the words. He also excelled at *processing* the information he gathered. He was able to gather the details and compose a strong and cogent case for his client.

However, what he failed to do was to complete the cycle and *respond* to his client. Being a fine attorney, he might argue that responding to his client was *not* his job.

On the other hand, if he had responded competently, he would have ensured the information he was getting was indeed what the client intended to communicate, and he would have provided some badly needed peace of mind for his client. This is not necessarily part of the lawyer's job description. Some might even see this as an extra.

I call it *added value.* Anyone in retail sales will tell you there is much to be said about providing added value to your product. And responding in a way that allows the speaker to know he or she has been heard is tremendous added value, no matter what business you're in.

REFLECTIVE RESPONSE REQUIRED

You will recall responding is the third component of powerful listening. It is the completion of the cycle, and deep, powerful listening requires this entire process.

In a combustion engine, the piston moves up the cylinder to its apogee where the spark ignites the fuel. The force of the combustion drives the piston down, and then it repeats the cycle. Each step of the process is vital to the function of the motor, and, in the same sense, each of the components of the listening cycle is essential.

Active, reflective, empathic (ARE) listening requires a response, and it is equally important as sensing and processing. The quality of the response has a strong bearing on successful listening. The attorney failed to respond, leaving the cycle incomplete.

Responding is what we also call reflecting. It is the *response* part of active, reflective, empathic listening. Simply put, it means to *reflect* back what you, the listener, hear the speaker saying.

Just as a mirror reflects what is in front of it, you—the listener—will reflect back what the speaker is trying to say. When you look in a mirror, it doesn't tell you w*hat* to wear, or that you look handsome, pretty, or even downright ugly today. It just reflects what is there. The same is true of reflective listening.

The original prototype of the *Law and Order* TV series is an old classic show called *Dragnet*. The story was about a couple of detectives in Los Angeles. One of the detectives would interview an eyewitness about the events at the crime scene. He would frequently repeat the last word or two of whatever the witness just finished saying. For instance, if the person said, "I saw two bank robbers come out of that door and take off in a black car," the detective would repeat "black car."

With that little cue, the person would continue recounting the event. All he needed was to hear a word or two of what he had just said in order to prompt him to continue telling his story. *That* is the way it is with reflective listening.

You might completely paraphrase what the speaker just said, or you might use a responsive sound, such as a *hmm* or *uh-huh*. This is called paralanguage, and reflective listening is simply listening with your voice and audibly sending the message *I got it.*

WHY DO IT?

Restated words and phrases, or reflective sounds, complete the perception, processing, and responding cycles of ARE listening. When we reflect or respond to the speaker, we are sending three messages: I hear *what* you're saying, I understand *what* you're saying, and I understand (or am trying to understand) *why* you feel that way.

People are often uncomfortable at first when I teach them how to listen reflectively. Let's face it, when you first begin to paraphrase what people say to you, it really feels awkward. It is hard work at the beginning, and one needs to always keep in mind there really is a payoff for the effort.

Reflective listening allows the speaker to know he or she is being heard. Besides, it ensures I have "sensed" correctly, and it ensures that the information I am getting is the correct information. If this were the only reason for reflective listening, it would be enough. But wait, just as with the late-night TV infomercial, *there's more!*

Many problems have no solution. At first glance, this might seem like a cynical statement, but recall that "just being heard" is crucial for conflict resolution and mediation.

A lot of problems have no solution except when they are "heard" by the other party. The act of listening out loud, with my voice, lessens the severity of the conflict and allows it to diminish and often dissolve.

The speaker might not experience any resolution to the problem, but being heard increases her ability to live with the unresolved problem to the extent it feels as if the problem has been fixed.

Responding by reflective listening ensures the speaker you got the message right to begin with. It affords her the chance to say, "Yes, that's exactly right" or "No, that's not what I'm saying."

It's better to get feedback in the moment and correct your misunderstanding than to get the wrong message and discover your mistake a day, a week, or a month later when the problem has gotten a lot worse.

When your pharmacist is filling your prescription, you don't want him guessing what your doctor scribbled on the prescription pad. If there is any doubt, you want him to call the doctor right then and verify the dosage. When pilots are speaking to air traffic control, they repeat the instructions they hear back to the tower. When the doctor says "*scalpel,*" the surgical nurse places it firmly in his hand and repeats "*scalpel.*"

These are professions where not getting the information right is a matter of life and death.

For you, the consequences of a misunderstanding might not be so dire, but research clearly demonstrates (for example, in retail sales) the person with the ability to reflect or mirror what he hears back to the potential customer is more successful.

Good salespeople understand their customers, and understanding does not take place unless the cycle of sensing, processing, and responding is complete. A mediator hears and repeats back what the party initiating the complaint is saying. This allows for clarification and sets the stage for meeting in the middle and finding common ground.

GET IT RIGHT!

Reflective listening helps the speaker get it right. Some of us figure out life by retreating into momentary solitude and spending time alone until we make sense of it all. Other folks figure out their issues by talking through them.

You enable people to hear their own words in a way they can make sense out of their thoughts when you give them the gift of reflecting their words back.

When I prepare a presentation, I use a dry-erase board to outline my thoughts and chart the course for what I want to say. I can do this process in my mind all day long, but until I externalize it—by getting it out of my head and on a wall somewhere—I can't make good sense out of it. It always seems to fall into place once it is out on the board, because it provides visual feedback for my brain.

In the same way, when we repeat people's words back to them, we've ostensibly become their verbal dry-erase board. We are providing a place where they can put their words and see their own thoughts from a different perspective. We do this without editing, advising, italicizing, or preaching. We simply give them back their words, believing they have the capacity within themselves to figure out the solution on their own.

THE POWER OF REFLECTIVE LISTENING

Psychologist Carl Rogers passionately believed people could find the answers to their problems if they were heard. He discouraged advice-dispensing, such as a "Dear Abby" approach. Instead, his tack was, "How can I listen to this person in a way that enables him to solve his own problem?"

Our training as therapists with tornado victims came from that same school of thought: "Don't advise them, don't try to fix them, and don't try to tell them how to feel." Instead, we were trained to take what prominent trauma expert Judith Herman called the "compassionate witness approach."

Our role as psychotherapists was just to "witness" what they were saying. A compassionate witness listens to what has been said and, by paraphrasing it back, assures the speaker, "Yes, this did happen to you" and "Yes, it is as terrible as you think."

You might be tempted to believe this would make them sink deeper into the pool of self-pity and victimhood. Some listeners are fearful if they listen in this way, they will precipitate this downward spiral.

Actually, the sooner you can go down into that dark place with the speaker, the more you empower him to begin to find his way up and out. What actually happens is the compassionate witness listens and affirms what he hears, and the speaker experiences the reality of the situation and the realization that, as bad as it was, he *survived* to tell his story.

This "telling it out loud" enables the speakers to marshal their own resources for moving forward, and most often after being "heard" out loud, that is exactly what they do.

The most powerful aspect of reflective listening and probably the least understood or mentioned is the deep bond of trust and connection established between speaker and listener when the listener reflects the speaker's words back to him or her.

HOW DO YOU DO IT?

On the grade-school playground during recess, there was always a mass jump-rope game going on. There would be two children, each twirling his or her respective end of the rope, and a line of kids impatiently waiting to jump in and strut their stuff. I was always a little intimidated by jumping in while the rope was turning. However, I was frequently amazed that when I *did* step through the moving rope, I found myself in the lime-light, jumping in front of all my friends. One moment I was on the outside, fearful, and the next moment I was doing what I feared.

Learning to be a good reflective listener is something like jump rope. You simply jump in and do it! You begin where you are, and, clumsy and awkward as it might seem, you just do it. And, *as* you do it, you will find yourself getting better.

A good place to start is to become aware of how often we respond without "reflecting." When someone speaks to us, we—without even thinking about it—move to answer, or to advice-giving, mode.

As you finish reading this chapter, pause and prepare yourself by "rehearsing" how you will interact with someone. In your mind, see them either asking you a question or stating how he or she feels or thinks about someone or something. Now see yourself intentionally pausing and, before you answer, formulating a simple reflection.

Try to go through your day, and every time someone speaks to you, repeat this ritual: pause before answering and take a moment to reflect or restate his words before responding to him. Even if the other person asks a question, before answering the question, reflect his words back.

TRAINING WHEELS

You probably had training wheels when you started learning how to ride a bicycle as a child. The training-wheel counterpart for reflective listening would be using prompts such as, "It sounds like..." or "I'm hearing you say..." or "You're telling me..."

These statements are a great way to get started: if you were trying to practice active listening, you might say, "It sounds like you're telling me that if I will use these at the beginning of a reflection, it will make it easier to get in the habit of reflecting." And to that I would answer, "That's correct. You got the message!"

Training wheels are good to get you started. Our goal, however, is to get you to a point where you do this so well that you don't need to use the "it sounds like" or "I'm hearing" or "you're telling me."

A reflective paraphrase is not a word-for-word repetition. We don't want to sound like a recording or a parrot. We merely want to present a word sketch of what we have just heard. Important components of communication are the way we deliver our reflective words, the pitch, the loudness, the inflection, the intensity of the vocabulary, and the speed of the words.

Words themselves account for only 7 percent of communication, but the paralanguage, or the *way* we say it, accounts for 38 percent of communication. Therefore, *how* we reflect is of more importance than *what* words we use to reflect.

PARALANGUAGE AND RESPONSIVE SOUNDS

Sometimes we don't have the opportunity to get a paraphrase into the conversation. A person can get caught up in telling the story without any pauses, and you might be interrupting if you try to paraphrase. Try reflecting with paralanguage:

153

uh-huh or *hmmm* or *oh!* Or try short word reflections, such as "wow," "I see," "tell me more," "that's awful," "that's great," or "that's interesting."

These are responsive words and sounds used along with paraphrasing. They assure the speaker you're getting the message. They are a way of allowing the speaker to know she can safely move through her story because you have accurately "heard" what she has said up to this point. In contrast, if she doesn't believe she has been heard, she will either shut down or circle back and tell the story again. Either way, the end result prevents her from getting where she needs to go.

Also, the reflective response encourages the speaker to delve deeper into the topic by prompting the eyewitness to move farther back into her memory and pull out more details.

It is amazing to observe a conversation where the listener is using good reflective listening, because the speaker seldom realizes what is taking place. Instead, the listener's reflection allows the speaker to move deeper into her own narrative. This action provides such a comforting and secure feeling that it beckons the speaker to relax and speak from the heart, all the while oblivious to what is actually taking place.

As you begin to practice reflective listening, you will probably feel a little clumsy, but chances are, very few people will notice. If they look at you strangely, just tell them you are really trying to be a better listener and honor people by giving them your full attention. Most folks will appreciate your intentions and go on with their story.

Reflective listening is just like jumping rope or ballroom dancing. You can read about it all day, but you don't start learning until you start doing it. And, as you begin to do it, just relax and be present with the speaker.

I have taught this skill in many workshops. I will introduce the topic and then get someone to just talk to me. All the while, I will be reflecting back what he is saying. I will stop after a period of time and ask the speaker if he was aware of what I was doing while he was talking. Often, the speaker will get a puzzled look on his face, and finally I will tell him I was reflecting his words. He instantly realizes this and is surprised.

When you reflect, you provide a means for the speaker to get deeper into his or her thoughts.

Remember, the *more* effectively you reflect, the *less* others become aware you're even there. You're providing a mental dry-erase board and, by reflecting, you're taking notes for them so they don't have to. This frees them to delve deeper into their own story.

WHAT *NOT* TO DO

I am one who believes men and women are equal yet wired very differently. As a man, I am wired to go into "fix-it" mode when someone comes to me with a problem. This isn't a character flaw. It is just part of the way we, as men, are wired.

If someone tells me "I have a flat tire," my natural response is "let's go fix it." It takes a lot more work to fix something for someone than it does to just acknowledge the reality of the situation. Not fixing or not giving advice would sound more like this:

"Oh man, I just went out to my car and saw that I have a flat tire."

"Your tire is flat? That is such a hassle!"

You will probably end up helping him change his tire. But, with this response, you have put "Mr. Fix-it" in the backseat and "Reflective Response" in the driver's seat. You must resist the urge to fix the problem or move into advice-giving mode. Drifting off into advice-giving and fixing feels *disrespectful* to the speaker.

When I believe I need to correct the listener, I am—whether I intend to or not—saying: "You don't know what's good for you. I need to step in and help you." When this occurs, I'm fixing. Most of the time, this isn't received well.

The speaker needs to feel like you respect his ability to find the way through his own thoughts.

Reflection is all about economy of words, so when you reflect, try to say as *much* as you can with as *few* words as you can. A short reflection encourages the speaker to continue on with his thoughts. He will get derailed, anxious, distracted, or just give up the conversation if he has to wait for you to pontificate before he can resume his train of thought. So don't go on and on and on and on…

BUT WHY?

When your child was two years old, his or her favorite word was probably "no!" When he or she reached the age of four, the favorite phrase was probably "but why?"

We never unlearn this habit and, as adults, we often respond to the speaker's thoughts by asking "Why?" But using this particular word tends to inhibit the speaker's thought process and weighs down the conversation. When tempted to use "why," try using "what" instead; for example, "What about this makes you feel this way?" or "What about this makes you believe that?" rather than "*Why* do you feel this way?"

Asking "Why?" and questions that require a yes or no response tend to shut the speaker down. "What?" and open-ended questions move the speaker forward.

Don't forget paralanguage as you reflect. Use *mmm-hmm*s and *uh-huh*s and monitor your tone. Don't let your response get too high or too fast. Try to keep a sense of calm in your voice. You are leading the speaker to a comfortable place where he will say what he needs to say. When you rush your answers, you will communicate impatience or, even worse, anxiousness in regard to his story. Don't mumble your reflections. Slow down and articulate clearly. The speaker needs to hear his words from your lips.

SOME DANGERS TO AVOID

While you might have to start out with training wheels, don't use them any longer than necessary. You want to move away from the stereotyped phrases people use to facilitate reflection, such as "I'm hearing you say" or "You're saying that." If you perceive the speaker is feeling sad, drop the "I'm hearing you" and just state, "You're sad." Or, if the speaker is saying she believes she is about to get fired, just state it: "You're afraid you are going to be fired."

PRETENDING TO UNDERSTAND

As with body language, you can't fake interest. So if you get distracted or lost in conversation, just stop the speaker and tell her, "I didn't get that. Could you repeat that again?" This will help you refocus and will also prevent your lapse of attention from making a poor impression on the other person.

Remember, the best time to right a wrong is when it happens. Admit you got distracted, say you're sorry, and move on with the conversation.

OVERREACHING

Don't try to ascribe psychological meaning or interpretation to the speaker's words or actions. If the person needs a psychologist, send him or her to a professional. Your job is to just be there with him and hear him. Trying to analyze the problem opens the door for "Mr. Fix-it" to sneak in and shut the conversation down by offering a quick solution.

UNDER-REACHING, MISSING IT

You need to stop and refocus if, in the course of reflecting, you find yourself repeatedly missing the feelings the speaker conveys or making responses that understate them. You'll know if you are doing this because the speaker will tell you, "No, that's not what I'm saying." Three of these strikes in a row, and you'll probably be out. If that happens, just stop and say, "For some reason I am not following you. Could we start over?"

BASIC PRINCIPLES OF REFLECTIVE LISTENING

You have two ears and one mouth…use them proportionately! Spend a lot more time listening than talking. Monitor your reflections, and don't pontificate!

Don't give very long or complex reflections. Short, simple responses are more effective. It is easy to go "on and on" and not even realize you have done it. Learn to focus in on the personal part of the speaker's message. You're listening to his "what's in it for me" messages, and you want to reflect on those as much as you can. For example:

> *Speaker: "My boss is really being a jerk lately. He insists on micromanaging the entire office staff's work. He is such a control freak, and it is just hurting our business."*

> *Listener: "The way your manager is behaving really bothers you. You're worried about how it will affect your job."*

At times, the speaker will say, "No, that's not what I meant. What I am trying to say is…" If this happens more than once, pause, get your bearings, close out as many distractions as you can, and refocus on the speaker.

As you home in on the content of the speaker's narrative, try to listen for his feelings and put these ahead of the facts. Often a narrative of facts is loaded down with a lot of feelings. Unpacking the feelings and reflecting them back will often result in the speaker saying, "That's right! That's exactly what I'm feeling." You will often hear words or paralanguage from him that infers discovery, insight, or the satisfaction of being heard and understood for once.

FOCUS!

- **Reflect what the speaker is saying about himself or herself.** They are talking about work, their boss, and their projects. But what they are really talking about is *how* they fit in that picture. Look for the connection to them.

- **Reflect back at the same level as the speaker.** Accept and clarify what the speaker is saying at his or her level. If she wants to talk about something really deep, don't try to lighten the conversation, as she will feel invalidated.

  When a coworker is bereaved about a loved one, most of us want to change the conversation, or at least lighten it up a little bit. Resist this urge and instead reflect back at that same level of emotional content. This allows the speaker to process her feelings and then move back toward more pleasant conversation.

  People need to speak about their experiences. Either we will provide that safe place for them to do this, or they will move on to someone else.

- **Reflect back feelings that are unexpressed but clearly implied by the speaker.** If she is all around the emotion of being excited but doesn't actually use the word, call it what it is: "You are really excited about that new sports car!"

- **Reflect back the speaker's ambivalent and negative feelings as well as the positive.** When we are trying to listen and reflect, our own alter ego, "Mr. Fix-it," is still trying to work in the background. He doesn't like to have to deal with problems, the messy stuff in life. When "Fix-it" is trying to get out, you will find yourself avoiding the speaker's negativity. Instead, maximize the speaker's positive thinking. Trying to steer him away from the negative will just cause him to circle back and go there even more. Often the speaker is verbalizing ambivalent feelings: "I really want to go on that cruise, but I'm not sure about taking off at that time, and I don't really have as much in savings as I'd like, but that cruise sure sounds good." My temptation, or Mr. Fix-it whispering in my ear, drives me to say, "Go on, take the vacation!" when I should just reflect, "It's really hard for you to make up your mind about this vacation."

If you take up ballroom dancing, you'll probably find that at first you are looking down at your feet and trying to count and stick with the pattern you have memorized. You might be picturing the little diagram your dance instructor gave you at the beginning of the session. As you get better at it, you'll spend less time counting, referring to the diagram, and making sure you do the steps just right, and instead you'll discover yourself just dancing more of the time.

So it is with reflective listening. At first, you will be very self-conscious. In time, however, you'll find yourself "dancing in the moment" with the speaker. Beneath the paraphrasing, the inflections, the *hmmms* and the *uh-huhs*, you will find that you are connecting with another human being and providing a place where he can safely express his thoughts and completing the cycle of communication in a way that is satisfying for both of you.

You will feel you have helped someone, and he will feel important, cared for, valued, heard, and empowered to solve his problems on his own.

WHAT IT DOES

Reflective listening can be powerful. There is tremendous power in hearing my own words. When I speak something out loud and someone paraphrases it back to me, it is like getting something out on the table where I can actually see it clearly for the first time.

As I type a manuscript on my computer, it is difficult for me to be objective about what I'm writing until I print it out. I can see it on the monitor and read right past all kinds of glaring errors. When I have the manuscript, I can hold my own words in my hands and *really* look them over.

This is what we provide when we reflect. We put people's own words back into their hands where they can figure out what needs to be done *without* our advice.

When you are listening and responding reflectively, you are helping the speaker increase his or her own processing power. If you could connect another computer with your own in order to combine and amplify the processing power, it would increase your computer's speed and ability to work equations.

By "reflecting," we are loaning part of our computing power to the speakers' brains by "holding" their thoughts for them. Reflecting the thought back out loud enables them to look at their own thoughts and see the wisdom or the fallacies of what they are saying. We become that dry-erase board where they can write out all the details and step back and take a look at their own thinking process.

ARE YOU TRYING TO TURN ME INTO A PSYCHOLOGIST?

We have encouraged you to use the listening model that ther-apists use. This doesn't necessarily mean we are trying to make everyone into psychotherapists. While the occupation might be different, the principles of powerful listening are the same.

You listen to help ensure you *understand* speakers' thoughts, and you are listening to help them understand their own thoughts, whether you are helping people solve deep problems in their life or just having coffee and listening to a friend ex-press her frustrations about a coworker.

As you listen, you share a common tool with the mental health profession, *and* the aviation industry, *and* with salespeo-ple, *and* doctors, lawyers, and a host of other professions.

WHAT'S IN IT FOR ME?

What's the payoff if you are going to the trouble of putting on the training wheels of reflective listening, exposing your clumsy attempts at listening, placing yourself at the mercy of the speaker, and risking humiliation and embarrassment? How will *you* benefit from becoming a great reflective, responsive listener?

People will feel drawn to you. If you want to be the life of a party, try this. Resolve beforehand you are just going to listen and reflect. You will find people are charmed by you and will remember you as the most interesting person of the evening. People will find they like you, although they might not know exactly why. You will—without fixing, advising, or telling—help people figure their own issues out.

When I teach workshops on listening, I introduce a little activity called "Summarize That!" For three minutes the partici-pants pair up, and one listens to the other talk about something he or she is excited about. The listener then has to summarize what he or she just heard the speaker say.

I always hear participants relate they would have listened better if they had known in advance what I was going to ask them to do.

You will find yourself becoming a much better listener when you know you are going to be paraphrasing someone's words. You will find yourself listening with your mind, and, as you learn to listen deeply, you'll become a better person because you will become increasingly "other-centered." This is a good place to be!

OBJECTIONS TO REFLECTING

There are always people who are wary about jumping in and trying something new. There are those who are cynical or just uncertain about reflective listening. There are always people who count the cost, or the price, of learning to listen reflectively and cite all the reasons *not* to do it.

Some of these are:

- **"I don't have time to listen to my employees whine about stuff."** A CEO told me recently he didn't have three hours to listen to one of his employees gripe about something. I said, "I'm not asking you to spend hours and hours listening to your people. I'm just suggesting that when you are required to listen, you listen intently, and listen well."

- **"I will spend my entire day just listening to one person. It is just a waste of time."** True, and true. Someone is communicating, and you fail to hear something important, which results in losing an employee. The cost of replacing that person is far more than the expense of occasionally spending a few minutes of your time to hear an employee talk something through. It certainly does take more time to stop and listen, but it saves time too. In the big picture, it avoids miscommunication, the ensuing problems, and the time required to correct the mistake.

It ensures the person feels heard, and it provides a check for errors in receiving the message.

- **It just sounds weird, and I feel awkward.**
  Yes, it does feel awkward at first, but the same was probably true for learning to ride a bicycle, or swimming, or driving a car. It takes some time and practice to reach a level where you can reflect naturally, but so do most skills. Reflect a little back of what you hear in every conversation, and you will get better at it. Besides, most people won't notice, because it just feels so good to have someone really hear you.

- **If I do this, won't it sound like "Polly want a cracker?"**
  Yes, you might sound like a parrot. But after a few tries, you will get better, and the person that you "parrotized" will probably not spend the rest of their life making fun of your attempt to be a better person. Even when you do sound like a parrot, most people will be so engrossed in their story they probably won't notice.

- **I don't have the time or energy to be the sounding board for all my employees.**
  Being available to others to vent does consume a lot of time, and ARE listening is hard work. It takes time, and it *does* drain you.

  But don't forget that the number-one reason why employees leave their place of work is because they are unhappy with their boss. Being "heard" makes people feel important. If they feel important, they will behave accordingly.

  Part of your job as a manager is to manage people. Listening skillfully is managing and, again, you cannot afford not to listen. Besides, when someone is able to get something off his chest, it enables him to return to his world and focus on his work, without the distractions of being emotionally distraught.

SUMMARY

Sensing, processing, and responding complete the cycle of listening, and listening with your voice completes the process. In order to truly listen, you must do all three. For most of us, responding appropriately is probably the most difficult part of the endeavor. I would encourage you to make a commitment to becoming a lifelong responder. Don't expect to become a reflective listener overnight, or this week, or this month. Rather, make a commitment to becoming a lifetime student of reflective listening. It is an investment that pays big dividends!

The attorney in the opening vignette might not win more cases if he became a more reflective listener, but he would certainly become a better person, and a person who really cares about his clients. On second thought, that might just make him a better attorney as well.

ACTIVITIES: PRACTICE LISTENING WITH YOUR VOICE

1. A good place to start is just to become aware of how often we respond without "reflecting." When someone speaks to us, we move to answer or advice-giving mode without even thinking about it. As you finish reading this chapter, pause and prepare yourself by "rehearsing" how you will interact with someone. In your mind, see that person either asking you a question or stating how he or she feels or thinks about someone or something. Now see yourself intentionally pausing and, before you answer, formulate a simple reflection.

2. Practice reflecting in every conversation (even very short ones).

   Yes, it takes some time and practice to reach a level where you can reflect naturally, but so do most skills. If you reflect back a little of what you hear in every conversation, you will get better at it. Besides, most people won't notice, because it feels so good to have someone really hear you.

3. Follow the "ground rules" of good listening:
   - ☐ Don't interrupt.
   - ☐ Don't change the subject or move in a new direction.
   - ☐ Don't rehearse in your own head.
   - ☐ Don't interrogate.
   - ☐ Don't teach.
   - ☐ Don't give advice.

4. Make a lifetime commitment to paraphrasing.
   Every time someone speaks to you—whether it is a statement or a question—first paraphrase a little of his or her statement before you respond with an answer.

5. Self-talk: Remind yourself what the speaker has to say is far more important than anything you could tell him or her.

Chapter Nine

LISTEN WITH YOUR MIND

"I waited while you spoke,
I listened to your reasoning;
while you were searching for words,
I gave you my full attention..."
Job 32:11-12

LISTENING TO MY WIFE—AN OLD STORY

Saturday mornings are magical at our house: coffee with my wife, relaxing, reflecting on the week, and sharing our dreams for the future. Throughout our many years of marriage, I have never ceased to be amazed at the new facets I learn about her. We've logged innumerable hours of heart-to-heart conversations and, by now, I think I ought to know this person very well.

Yet recently, on one of those perfect Saturday mornings, I learned something I never knew before. I asked her what in her life story makes her unique as a counseling therapist. She explained when she was eight years old, her family was in a bad car accident, and she was hospitalized for two weeks with a broken jaw. I knew about the wreck, but I didn't know the rest of the story.

Hospitals were different in 1962. They just weren't fun places for a child to be. Back in those days, no *kid* visitors were allowed. She is one of five children who spent most of their waking hours together, and now she was suddenly isolated from her brothers and sisters.

For the first three days, she shared a room with her injured mother. The downside of having four siblings is it makes individual attention a scarcity, so having her mommy all to herself was a real treat.

After mom was released on day three, a cranky old lady became her new roommate for a day or so, and then, my wife—the little girl—was all alone in her big room in the hospital.

The nurses, seeing that she was lonely, gave her special treatment. They played with her during their breaks or any free moments. Throughout her stay she was showered with toys. Many of those were paper dolls. The nurses had a grand old time helping her cut out and dress her paper dolls. They focused on her and pampered her through her recovery.

Her normal life at home required competing with the litter for her parents' attention, but here she got a taste of being very special. She could see the contrast between competing with the crowd and having someone focus intently on you.

This gave her a deep understanding of how powerfully healing that type of focused attention can be. She observed this is part of what has made her successful in her counseling practice. She gets it. She understands what it's like to be heard, and she understands what it's like to be lost in a crowd and *not* heard. She has a special place in her heart for hurting people who grew up starving for attention. It was her childhood hunger to be known, to be understood, that shaped her thinking and her approach as a therapist.

Here, I thought I knew everything about her, and yet, after these many years together, she managed to pull out a new story. As we sat there basking in the morning sun, enjoying the aroma of fresh-brewed coffee, I listened with my mind. I *saw* her story like a movie in my head, the drab institutional green of hospital walls of the early '60s; the cold, skeletal, white metal hospital beds; and the nurses with their little white hats, aprons, and perfectly starched dresses. I could see their white stockings and clunky shoes. The institutional smells from a half-century earlier flooded my mind. The solvents and disinfectants, partly used to mask the other smells, were strong in my head. I saw the checkerboard squares of linoleum under my feet. I heard the chatter of kind women playing with a sweet little girl. I heard their laughter as their dolls carried on unlikely and outlandish conversations. I was there in the room, I was touched, and I was moved to tears by the experience.

In that magic moment of clarity, I *listened with my mind*. I didn't set out to see a video of her experience in my head. It just happened, because it was a culmination of all the other skills. I was relaxed and not preoccupied with something else, and I was focused on hearing the answer to my question.

This is *listening with your mind*. It only occurs when you are relaxed and patient, open with your body, at peace, and yet at once active. In this place you are able to reflect and draw from a plentiful reservoir of patience. When you reach this point, you have set the stage for listening with your mind, which is much more than just listening with your brain.

Your mind uses your brain, but your mind is far bigger. If your brain is the computer, your mind is the person sitting at the keyboard. Your mind is not limited to your brain or even your body. You hear, you process, you respond with your brain. It is like the automated response telephone system so many companies use: You call. A computer talks to you. It has no feeling. It just does what you tell it to, unless you confuse it by pressing the wrong buttons.

Your mind is so much more than just your brain. Your mind moves beyond the boundaries of your head and, like water, it flows and mingles with other minds in close proximity. Your mind is the part that empathizes and connects with others.

When we interact with another person, we link two "computers" together to provide more processing power to solve a problem.

If you're a science-fiction buff, you might remember Mr. Spock on "Star Trek" and the Vulcan mind-meld—"*Your thoughts are my thoughts...your feelings are my feelings.*" Science fiction *didn't* invent this.

Melding of minds occurs with powerful listening and creates a level of intimacy many people long for, but few attain. It is the mind-meld of intimacy, where one becomes so caught up in what another is saying the listener vicariously experiences what he or she hears or at least sees the images in his or her mind.

This action builds a deep connection between friends and even deeper intimacy between lovers. When we engage others at this level, we experience relationships in an entirely new and satisfying dimension. When we consider the benefits of deep listening, enhanced intimacy is one of the many perks of taking the time and energy to listen with your mind.

We have covered the types of listening, the physiology of listening, the three components of listening, and the steps for good listening. We put it all in an easy-to-remember acronym: ARE listening. These are the mechanical parts of good listening.

Knowing them doesn't make you a good listener any more than knowing all the engineering principles required to build a fine car makes you a professional racecar driver. You can know all this and *still* not be a good listener. These are the steps that get you *to* good listening.

But there is a transformation that takes place when you move from knowing what to do and going through the steps to actually *doing, listening,* and *engaging* another human being at an incredibly deep level. This is powerful listening or *listening with your mind.* It is where your mind links with someone else's, and you can *feel* what they are feeling and *see,* and *smell,* and *experience* it with your senses.

However, most of us aren't born with the ability to listen well, and we don't get it by osmosis or through our genes either. Instead, it requires intentional, mindful practice. You go through the steps until it becomes second nature and then, one day, you find that you are really listening in a wonderful way.

This is why the Department of Labor recommended adding listening expertise to the core skills in our national educational curriculum. It is a skill, as with playing a musical instrument, best mastered when the student begins the process at a young age and practices often.

BALLROOM DANCING

A few years ago, we saw an ad in the newspaper for a ballroom dancing class. It consisted of five lessons and a dance party for a package rate. We decided to take the plunge and enroll.

I remember the first lesson. They brought out a diagram and showed us the fox-trot: *forward, forward, left, left,* or for my wife, *backward, backward, right, right.* We learned the tango, the West Coast Swing, and my favorite, the waltz: *forward, side, back, together*...With those maps in our heads, we were ready to hit the dance floor and show off our moves. How shiny we looked at parties with our steps coordinated. I am rhythmically challenged, but as long as I could count the steps, I could fake it pretty well.

As we practiced dancing, or what I *thought* was dancing, I eventually reached a point where I was able to stop counting out loud, or just counting at all, and go with the flow and truly *dance.* When you reach that special moment in the Zen of dancing, you've made the switch, and you know it. The shift from just going through the steps to that instant when you really begin dancing is as different as night and day.

One is focused on the mechanics of the action, and the other is delighting in motion.

Our goal is to get you to where you are listening without even thinking about listening or being so caught up in what you hear you're seeing a movie of the event in your mind. Does it happen automatically? Yes, at times, and no at other times.

Most of us get to the art of listening well by just doing the steps over and over until what is mindful becomes natural. We begin the process by becoming aware of our deficiencies. Then we become aware of what we need to do, or we aren't doing. Then we begin to succeed part of the time, but we are acutely aware of how forced and unnatural it feels. And, finally, in a wonderful moment of discovery, we realize we are listening well.

It's a process like learning to dance. You practice the moves and refine your steps until you become proficient.

PRIMING THE PUMP

However, there is a way to prime the pump of the mind so the pictures start taking shape sooner and more often in the conversation.

During Sunday sermons, my mind has a tendency to wander far from the preacher's homily, so I have resorted to doing something I did as a child: drawing during preaching. My childhood pew-art consisted of guns, tanks, and wars. I drew the stuff of a little boy's world.

As an adult, I try to draw whatever the preacher is communicating. I go from notes, to stick drawings, to doodles, to the parted Red Sea and sheep in a pasture. I focus on the sermon by drawing what I hear.

I use part of this technique for listening to people. I get out the imaginary flipchart in my head and begin to draw what I hear in conversations where there are a lot of distractions around me and I'm having a hard time trying to focus on the speaker. I try to see picture representations of the words I'm hearing. I can recall much more of the conversation because of my mental artwork.

Learning to draw pictures in your mind of what you hear is a wonderful way to make the transition from going through the steps of listening to actually listening with your mind. As you begin to cultivate this skill, you will soon find yourself "seeing" conversations without any effort at all. It just happens!

THE MIND MAP

Remember in grade school when your teacher would break the normal routine with an art project? They handed you a stack of magazines and told you to cut out pictures and paste them on a sheet of paper and make a collage: "Tell a story about yourself, your family, your vacation, and your dreams." Soon, you had a room full of budding Picassos pasting away and illustrating the events of their lives.

Children love to cut and paste their life stories. But as we grow up, we give up cutting and pasting when we shouldn't.

Apply this principle to skillful listening by visualizing pictures of what you hear. As you learn to listen in pictures, you are allowing the visual and artistic side of your brain to create a detailed collage of that person. See yourself cutting that very picture out of a magazine and pasting it on a collage in your mind.

This technique is really handy when I meet someone for the first time. I am often anxious to make a good impression or just self-conscious. As a result of my own distractions, I miss much of the first vital five minutes of the conversation.

I anticipate these moments and have the crayons of my mind poised and ready to begin to draw. I capture important information, and it becomes part of the collage for that person. If that person is married, I draw or paste a picture of the spouse in the picture. If he has teenagers, I draw him doing teen things. One's a singer? I draw her in the school chorale or doing an impersonation of the current heartthrob.

As you listen and compose images in your mind, add whatever details you hear to that picture. You'll be amazed at how much you recall the next time you see that person.

Remember the old adage "a picture is worth a thousand words?" We think in images, so this is the most efficient way to store information and, at once, enhance listening skills. It appears that these icons take up a lot less space on the hard drive of our brain and, for me, they seem a lot more accessible than just trying to remember details without the visual aids.

DIVIDENDS

The collage method or sketching a picture in your mind pays handsome dividends as well. For old acquaintances, the collage becomes a rich tapestry of colorful experiences and memories. When I think of friends, I immediately think of the pictures of the good times I've shared with them.

Deep listening facilitates this action. It is the process of creating a picture of everything about the other person. Not only do I see the details of the person's life story, but also I have reminders of his character, who he is, and what he stands for.

As you listen and get to know a person by "drawing" him, you create a reservoir of goodwill toward that person, because you know who he is and the history you have shared. Also, this enables us to see the good in others and look for the best possible explanation for their behavior.

All of this provides information for a mental database accessed when that person does something unexplained, something that could be interpreted as unkind or untoward. Without thinking about it, I compare his present actions to his history and character and conclude there must be a perfectly logical explanation for this behavior. My logic might follow something like, "I know that person. I don't know why he did what he did, but I know from past experience that he is a good person and there must be a good explanation for *why* he took that particular action."

Without the picture in our mind, we tend to interpret what others do in the most negative light. The detailed picture of that person in our mind is the antidote to negative interpretation.

BACK TO SATURDAY MORNINGS

Our Saturday morning ritual is the dividend for somehow learning to listen to each other early in our marriage. We develop an empathy and compassion for each other when we listen with our minds and really follow the speaker's train of thought.

Empathy is the ability to project oneself into the personality and the experience of another individual to better understand what that person is feeling.

When we cross over the divide into others' experience, we also experience deep intimacy. For lovers, this level of intimacy is called "oneness." This action provides the glue that holds a relationship together. Because we made the investment of listening with our minds, we have this rich resource to draw on when the relationship road gets bumpy, as it inevitably does. We have been able to weather the storms of life and continue dreaming together because we have learned to listen with our minds, to be drawn deep into the picture of each other's lives.

In a relationship—in *any* relationship—one of the elements that keeps things moving in a positive direction is when those who are in any relationship commit to truly listen to each other.

This is accomplished when you allow your mind to see the pictures, to participate in the artwork, and to vicariously "see" what the other person is trying to communicate, and understand with your mind what is coming from your heart.

The goal of listening with your mind is simply to listen effortlessly, without "counting the steps." Be carried away by the story so the experience in the speaker's mind becomes as real and vivid in the listener's mind as well.

Listening with your mind is truly a dance. You'll find yourself struggling at first to keep up with the steps and working hard to avoid stepping on each other's toes. But with time and practice, you'll find yourself waltzing with the best.

ACTIVITIES: PICTURES IN YOUR HEAD

1. Practice sketching what you hear when you're on the phone or listening to a lecture or seminar. Also, practice visualizing pictures of what people are saying. If you feel like you're artistically challenged, just draw caricatures or stick-figures. The point is to get pictures in your head.

2. Summarize this: when you meet someone for the first time, see how many facets of the person you can put in your mental picture in your initial conversation.

As you listen, remember to:
    1. Listen for facts as well as the feelings behind the facts.
    2. Identify the speaker's main points with a key word or phrase.
    3. Take brief notes while you listen.
    4. Constantly summarize the speaker's words by repeating key words in your mind.

Chapter Ten

LISTENING TO GOD

"Bidden or unbidden,
God is present"
Carl Jung

HEART LISTENING

Two paths get you to the back side of a barn. You can go around the left side, or you can go around the right side. Either way, the destination is the same.

We've spent the last nine chapters discussing *one path* of getting to the back side of the barn.

To become a powerful listener, getting around to the back side of the barn is ultimately learning to be so fascinated with another person that you become mesmerized by his or her words and drawn into his or her stories. It is the ultimate form of selflessness—being so focused on the other that you are not even aware of yourself. It is being fully present.

That's the destination. Getting there from one side is a methodical route, where one learns the types of listening, the physiology of listening, what to do, and what *not* to do, and practices a lot.

You may want to consider another route to get to the back side of the barn. This alternative path deals with listening and the spiritual side of who we are.

I am a tree-lover. I've planted more than a hundred pines on my acreage. I love their smell. I love that they are green all winter long. I love the sound the wind makes as it blows through their branches, and seeing them takes me on a momentary trip to the mountains.

A few years ago, an insect bored into the new young growth in the tips of the branches and attacked my pine trees. I could just imagine losing all of my beautiful pines, so I got out my insecticide and went to war, intent on eradicating the blight. But my efforts didn't seem to make any difference. The bugs went right on chomping my pines.

In desperation, I made a trip to the local nursery. I asked the resident horticulturalist what to do. He recommended using a systemic insecticide. He explained you apply it at the roots, where the poison is absorbed, and the entire tree becomes toxic to the borers. I followed his advice and treated the entire system. I was able to save my pines.

There is a systemic approach to listening as well. Rather than working on the behaviors of listening—the tips of the branches—why not approach the issues to promote good listening from the roots—the very essence of who we are, our values, our core beliefs, and the substance of our souls?

At the core of my roots is a deep and abiding faith in God. That's the path we will consider.

So if you're an atheist, you might want to skip this chapter. I don't have anything against people who don't have faith or belief in God, but if you don't believe in God, this chapter might be irrelevant for you.

There is one principle that effectively changes the way a person listens: learning the art of being silent and listening to God. This is the practice, the art, and the action that brings everything in listening together.

The systemic approach to becoming a powerful listener is like the systemic treatment for pines. Approaching listening from this path is applying something to the root that works its way through your system and has a profound impact on your entire being.

The systemic approach to becoming a great listener is to slow down and take the time to be silent and listen to—or for—God's voice. By learning to listen to God, you alter your *entire* system, and you will be better equipped to listen to people.

A quest in the scientific community is to find a unifying theory to explain everything in the universe. Researchers in particle physics seek to unlock the secret of how it all fits together or the central theme or principle that explains all that exists. This has been the grist that has fueled much debate in the scientific community.

Often, the Science television channel presents programs pitting the research and hypotheses of Einstein against Hawking.

It is intriguing for me to think of the possibility of one theory that explains everything in the universe. Wouldn't that be nice! That's the way my brain works.

While I can't answer the question at a subatomic level, I do believe that at the relationship level, the unifying theory of listening—the theory that makes everything else work—is perhaps learning to listen to God.

Now you might not hear God speak to you in an audible voice, and then again you might. However, I do recommend you consider taking time to be quiet, to ponder his universe, to listen for him.

We live in a world where technology is a constant distraction. There is an "app" for everything, and my problem with so many shiny, pretty things is not being able to decide which new toy I want to play with right now. With sensory overload getting the best of us, it's difficult to be still and hear anything. Is it any wonder we don't hear God? We get so busy there is no time to listen.

What would it be like to take the time to get quiet, and listen for God to speak to you?

The truth is we are really uncomfortable with silence. Perhaps our discomfort grows out of a fear that if we actually do get quiet, we might just hear the voice of God and, even worse, he might actually *ask* us to do something.

If we aren't willing to listen to the Almighty, why would we even consider listening to mere mortals? His spirit infuses us with his presence when we take the time to slow down, clear our mind, and make the time to listen to God. When this takes place, we are changed, and we begin to see people differently.

First, listening to God means just practicing being silent and being in the moment. The silence is the easier part. We can resolve not to talk without much problem. For most of us, having permission to go on a speaking hiatus might be welcomed.

But being in the moment and not pulling out your iPhone or doing something to entertain yourself is another story.

Do we reach for a magazine, go down our to-do list, or get out our laptop and *do* something when we find ourselves in a waiting area at the airport or in the reception area of someone's office? Funny thing, how we always *need* to be busy, never missing a moment to be productive, but only to an extent.

Our failure to pause and enjoy rest keeps our brains just this side of exhausted.

Do we really produce more by multitasking in the dentist's office? Are we really so efficient that we can, like the Energizer Bunny, go nonstop and not reap the consequences?

This state of constant busyness has become a part of our culture. We toss our children overboard into a sea of extracurricular activities, homework, and sports. As a consequence, there is never time for them just to think. We keep them going all the time, and they never have a moment to be introspective.

So when we look at ourselves and realize there is never a moment for reflection, we are just doing what most people think is normal. Or is it?

You'll probably be disappointed if you're expecting God to speak to you like thunder. The Old Testament characterizes his words as a *still, small voice*. I continue to hold out for the loud-speaker level of volume from a Charlton Heston-like voice for all to hear and settle the matter of his existence once and for all.

But what I have experienced over and over is his guidance in my life when I take the time to be quiet, slow down, and make room for him.

Listening to God means not filling every waking moment of our lives with activities and stuff but, rather, budgeting some time just to ponder.

My father-in-law was an aerospace engineer. He tackled some complex aviation problems during his career. He was also a farm boy and grew up attuned to the cycles of the seasons and not tuned in to TVs, radios, or technology.

As a result of his upbringing and experience of rural life, he was a quiet and often contemplative man. He took time to just to sit and ruminate. He pondered. At times he gave himself permission to do nothing except think.

I suspect for him, as well as for anyone who makes the time to ponder, he heard the voice of God. He was a man of integrity whose actions reflected well-thought-out values. His values were rooted in his faith in God, and his actions were aligned accordingly. He understood the importance of reflection.

How exactly do you listen to God? When you pray, do you go down a shopping list and check off what you want? Does your conversation with the Almighty seem to be mostly "Give me this" or "I really need that"?

Next time you pray, the moment you close your eyes—or whatever you do to begin your time of prayer—just be still in God's presence. Don't ask him for anything. Don't tell him anything. Instead, just "be" and be silent in his presence. Then, just focus on him and wait patiently for him to speak to you.

I have a lifelong friend with whom I get to spend extended time once or twice a year. He is a brilliant yet introspective person, and sometimes he can be quite reserved. At times, we might be visiting, and he will lapse into silence. Early on in our friendship, I felt like I needed to make conversation in those quiet moments. But, over time, I came to understand that he was OK with the silence, and I learned to accept silence as a part of our conversation. When we go camping together, we often just sit, in silence.

This is what God invites us to do—just sit, in silence, with him. Once God has our silence and our focus, we can invite him to speak to us.

In the Old Testament, a mother gave her little boy, Samuel, to a priest who lived in the temple to raise. Subsequently the boy was to serve God as an acolyte.

One night, the boy was sleeping next to the altar and heard someone calling his name. He got up and ran into the bedroom of the old priest (whose name was Eli) and said, "What do you need?" Eli answered, "I didn't call you," and he sent him back to bed.

This happened two more times that night before Eli finally realized it was God who was calling little Samuel.

The third time Samuel came to his room, Eli told him to go back and lie down, and if he heard the voice speak again, he was to reply by saying, "Speak, Lord, for your servant is listening."

This is what God wants from a person—to get quiet and to invite him to speak.

When we pray we should be doing exactly that. As we go through the moments of our day, we should take time to just invite him to be a part of what we're doing.

I don't hear God speak in an audible voice. But I do listen for that still, small voice that guides me and reminds me it isn't all about me but about something bigger than me.

In the Old Testament, the Psalmist wrote: "Be still and know that I am God" (Psalm 46:10). *Stillness* is key to the *knowing*. Perhaps we busy ourselves because we know if we slow down, we *will* hear the voice of God. I wonder if there might be fewer skeptics if the whole world took more time to be silent.

As a culture, we are driven to distraction. Our children are over-scheduled, over-stimulated, and expected to overachieve. Our action is to stay in motion, all the time. Our values drive what we do. We value success, getting ahead, being the best, and looking good. Those are what we value. We also value loyalty, altruism, taking care of the planet, not using hate-speech, and on and on. But where do these values come from?

If you believe in God, your values probably stem from a belief that the universe is the way it is because God made it that way. If your faith is in the government, you'll expect the government to take care of things. If your faith is in your fellow man, you'll expect him to always take the right action.

If your faith is in God, then you probably have a set of values predicated on his principles and provision. Let's look at some of those.

The book of Genesis is held in high regard by Muslims, Jews, and Christians alike. It states God created man in his own image.

As a child, my image of God was a dour old man with a long gray beard and bald head sitting on a stone throne at the top of a very austere set of stone steps. In that picture, the wind is blowing, the sky is dark and cloudy, and, in my mind, God's countenance is equally frightening.

The Bible states we're created in God's image. Is that what it means? Is he a really scary old guy with a long white beard? Does God have a body? Does this mean God has two arms, two legs, and a face?

Most theologians interpret *being created in God's image* as our sharing certain character qualities with God. We are created in his image. We are thinkers. God has a will. We, his creation, exercise choice. God has emotions. We feel. God is the creator. We have this need to create. God is love. We have this same capacity to love.

We are created in his image in that we reflect the nature of his character. We are like him.

But how about when I'm stuck in traffic and lose it and say something derogatory about the guy in the car in front of me? Good thing I have tinted windows. Or what about the times I'm fearful or fail at listening to others the way I should? How do I reflect the image of God in those times?

The problem is we are created in the image of God, but we live in a broken world or, as theologians call it, a "fallen" world. This is a place that in God's original design was intended to be perfect. We were created to be other-centered, caring, thinking creatures.

But sin happened and put a monkey wrench in the works. Our faith is in God at work, drawing us to him, and he is in the process of making peace with the world. Taking the time to listen attentively to God is a little part of joining him in the peacemaking process.

My worldview is God made us in his image. If this is true, then every one of us is an image-bearer. Each of us reflects something of the face of God, and each of us is a unique masterpiece with God's autograph in the corner.

The first time we went to France, we visited the Louvre Museum in Paris. No trip to the Louvre should be without a visit to the *Mona Lisa*. Problem is, although the room is huge, the *Mona Lisa* is a rather small painting, and everybody has the same idea: get as near to the painting as possible. As a result, there is always a crowd of people clamoring to get a close look at this masterpiece.

Everyone visiting Paris wants to see this famous work of art. Why? Because we understand it is a one of a kind, so we value it; we treasure it.

A painting by a man is considered a masterpiece. It can't *talk, think, do, love,* or *create anything*. Yet thousands of people flock to the Louvre every day, just to get a glimpse of this great painting.

We cross paths with human beings moment by moment and seldom stop to marvel at these *feeling, thinking, acting, doing, creating, capable-of-loving* masterpieces. They are truly unique masterpieces, and we fail to value them. In fact, if one of them makes us late for work, we regard them with disdain and contempt.

If our actions are informed by our values, and our values are informed by our belief in God, and our belief in God includes the belief we are created in his image, then image-bearers are all unique masterpieces. Do we treasure them as such? How do we cross paths with masterpieces that surpass the *Mona Lisa* and not stop to appreciate and admire what we experience?

If we believe all this, then we should act in a way that values image-bearers.

And how do we accomplish this? We do this by listening to them, by taking the time to pull out of the race and into a pit stop to spend the time focusing on another. In doing so, we honor God, their creator, and the master artist.

LOVE MY KIDS, LOVE ME

My sons are adults. I am very proud of the men they have become. They are making their own way in life and living with integrity and success. Every now and then, someone will tell me, "Hey, I met your son…he is really a great guy!" When this happens, I always feel myself drawn to that person. I really like people who like my kids. I am drawn to people who are kind to my kids. This shines light on a principle that all of us who have kids know full well. "If you love my kids, I'll love you" because loving my kids is like loving me, and all of us *love* to be loved.

The point here is if you say you really love God, prove it by loving what is valuable to him. His children are precious to him; he gave his very best for them just to prove it. If we value others, we honor him.

If God is anything like a good father, and if fathers are created in the image of God, then this instinctual proclivity to like people who like our kids must come from him. I imagine he is really pleased when we love and value his children by regarding them as important enough to take the time to listen to their hopes, dreams, and fears.

As we listen to God, something inside us changes. We gain a new perspective on his creation, and we begin to value what he values. We value him by listening to others, intently, actively, reflectively, and empathically.

Listening is good for business. Become a better listener, and your listening skills will have a positive impact on your business. Become a better listener at home, and you will see your relationships improve. You'll see a positive impact on your life.

However, there is a deeper reason to listen. We honor God when we listen to others. Listening makes a statement: *God, this person is made in your image. The way I can value them the most is by putting my agenda aside and focusing on listening to them in this moment.* In doing this, I'm loving what God loves and cherishing what God cherishes.

In the New Testament, Jesus talks about the way we treat people. He was commending some folks for giving him water when he was thirsty, feeding him when he was hungry, and providing clothing for him and visiting him in prison. The crowd responded, "When did we do this?" Jesus' response was, "When you did it to one of the least of these brothers." He was saying when you focus on and care for the marginalized of our society, it is tantamount to focusing on and caring for God.

It's easy to serve important people. We fall all over ourselves to be of service to someone important. But for the invisible ones, the folks that fade into a corner or live under a bridge— well, that's often a different story.

Imagine you get a call from the president or some well-known celebrity asking you to be a sounding board or a confidante. I know how I feel when someone important wants my help. It feels good when people take you into their confidence and bare their souls to you.

But our attentiveness is directly proportionate to the importance we give to the speaker. If it's someone we don't like or don't see as important to our advancement, how patient are we at listening to that person?

It is easy to overlook those who have no perceived importance in our lives. There are even those we avoid. You know—the person at work who is a chronic complainer, the person at church who always needs prayer for something, the guy on the street corner with the "I'll work for food" sign. These are the marginalized that appear to be hopelessly broken and beyond repair.

Or it may just be that quiet person who doesn't ever speak much, the one who comes to work every day and never has anything to say and blends into the background. The invisible man or woman in your life might not be in the hopelessly broken category; rather, he just isn't there. He is simply not a part of your life.

LISTENING TO THOSE WHO ARE SUFFERING

Something is wrong with the universe. Things tend to break. Stuff wears out. People hurt each other. They are insecure, weak, frail, broken, and needy. Everywhere you turn there is someone who seems to be hopelessly broken. These are "the least of these brothers," and as Jesus said, "taking care of them is like giving me a glass of water."

But they are the ones we often find the most difficult to listen to.

It is all too easy to simply avoid them and, if that's not possible, discount their words, marginalize them, or just pathologize them as not well adjusted. Then I come to my senses and realize what I'm doing, and I ask, "What's wrong with me? Why am I not more tolerant?"

I'm not sure it's actually a question of a character flaw. Instead, I believe it is something in the way we were made and our theology.

When it comes to "the least of these," listening is difficult because when we're exposed to the broken side of humanity, we avoid or turn away because we instinctively want to do something but we don't have that capacity. We are stifling our "Mr. Fix-it" mode.

We want to leave our handprint on life, a legacy. We want to make a difference; we want to be part of a solution.

But we quickly size up the situation and realize we don't have the power to fix them. There are just some situations beyond our ability to make a difference. We are faced with the impossibility of fixing what is irreparably broken, and then we realize they are beyond our power to fix. We pull away by quietly and discreetly, backing out of the picture.

I believe this is because we don't want to fail at what we see as an impossible situation. If we can't fix them, we don't want to be stuck with them. We are so bent on fixing people that we can't just "be" with people.

How sad we don't realize the one true gift we have, what might offer healing and hope, is simply listening to them.

Author Henri Nouwen said it best: "We ignore our greatest gift, which is our ability to be there, to listen, and to enter into solidarity with those who suffer." This act could easily appear to be a waste of time, but in actuality it is the *only* real fix we can provide.

By listening, we do become instrumental in the healing and mending process. When we begin to value what God values, when we will value "the least of these" and truly see them as signed and autographed masterpieces, how can we not listen to them actively, reflectively, and empathically?

We appropriate the unifying theory of listening when we take the other path around the barn by clearly understanding that when we embrace a systemic approach and take time to be silent and listen to God, he *will* show up and speak to us, and he will change our system from the roots up. Our priorities will change.

In listening to him, our internal systems will change as well. We'll become more other-centered. We will value those around us and have special compassion for the needy. Our listening capacity will be transformed. We will take pleasure in focusing on others, and it will happen because we've taken the systemic approach.

Listening to God changes all of who we are, from the inside out.

ACTIVITIES: LEARNING TO LISTEN TO GOD

1. Schedule time throughout your day to stop, clear your mind, and listen to God.

2. Carry a notebook. Keep a record of everyone who crosses your path on a daily basis. Spend some time at the end of the day thinking about each of them. Consider what makes them a unique masterpiece. The next time you see them, tell them what you see in them that you admire.

3. Ask God to help you see the "masterpiece" in each of his creations.

Chapter Eleven

WHAT DO I GET OUT OF THIS?

"If speaking is silver, then listening is gold."
Turkish Proverb

THE DIVIDENDS OF POWERFUL LISTENING

Her mommy and daddy were going out on a "date." She was *so* excited to have a new babysitter. This one was fourteen and, to a five-year-old, that is really grown-up. After her parents were gone, she and the babysitter baked cookies and had a real girl-to-girl chat. "What would you like to be when you grow up? asked the babysitter. The little girl responded, "A street walker, of course!" The babysitter was flabbergasted and more than a little put off by this response.

Later, when her parents returned from their night on the town, the babysitter mentioned this conversation to the parents as she registered her concern over the little girl's choice of future occupations. The mother responded without missing a beat. "Oh yes, she really does want to be a street walker. That's what she calls the crossing guards that walk out in the street to stop traffic so children can get to school safely."

I would imagine the babysitter might have reaped better dividends if she had listened carefully and asked clarifying questions. We're that way a lot of the time. We fail to listen and, as a consequence, we fail to enjoy the dividends of powerful listening.

What are the dividends of learning to listen well? You'll remember names and details of people's lives, you'll manage people better, and you'll find success in any task where working with others is required.

Finally, you'll find your significant other is pleased to enjoy the intimacy deep listening provides. The labor of mastering a task no longer feels like work when one can see the benefits of accomplishing it. I am always willing to invest time and energy in a project if I know it will pay big dividends.

NAMES

I have an associate who is an etiquette and protocol expert. She is called upon to work through the logistics and propriety when the president or someone high in government comes to town. She has a sobering statement printed on the back of her business card:

> *In the time it takes to read this card,*
> *You have made a first impression.*
> *Those seven seconds can last a lifetime.*

That's a pretty scary thought, but true. Have you ever found yourself immediately forgetting someone's name a moment after being introduced? What happens to that person's impression of me when it is clear that I can't remember his or her name? When we meet people for the very first time, we are often more focused on whether or not we might have a wardrobe failure, bad breath, look silly, or just make a poor impression. We miss what we *really* need to hear—their name.

How many times have you been introduced to someone, only to immediately forget his or her name? Or you were so preoccupied you really didn't hear the name when you were first introduced?

Our worries about making a good impression sometimes keep us from hearing important stuff, which you only get one shot at getting right. A consummate student of listening—always practicing the craft—will meet someone and take the opportunity to turn the focus away from himself and onto the speaker.

At an initial meeting, you need to have that marker and dry-erase board set up in your brain so you are ready to mentally take note of everything you hear. This will improve your ability to remember names and, not only will you remember names, but other details will quickly form a picture in your mind.

That first impression is a lasting one, and, if you're intently focused on the other person, that impression will most likely be a positive one.

By listening well, you learn a lot more about the other person in that short introduction. You'll have a very detailed picture of exactly who she is in just a few moments, and you will probably win a friend. Now that is a great benefit!

CONNECTIONS

As you will recall, my grandmother and grandfather owned a plumbing company. During the Great Depression, they lost everything and survived to tell about it. After the hard times were over, they worked the rest of their lives to recover. Long after my grandfather retired, my grandmother continued to run the business until she was in her eighties.

Having weathered the ups and downs of many business cycles, she developed a business savvy that was expressed in simple terms. She used to say, "You've got to do business with your friends, because your enemies sure won't do business with you."

Now that's about as simple as it gets, but true! You will most likely do business with friends, and friends are connections.

Listening to others creates deep bonds and connections. People feel very drawn to those who focus on them. If people are drawn to you and feel like they know you, they are more likely to do business with you. Most people who need a service or a product will ask a friend for a recommendation. My wife, the psychotherapist, advertises her business in the Yellow Pages, but the bulk of her business comes by word of mouth. New clients come to her primarily because other satisfied clients refer them. The chain of logic is "I know this person, I know she is reliable, and I know you will find that she is trustworthy and competent. I like her, so you'll undoubtedly like her too."

We introduce our friends to people with whom we feel comfortable and trust.

That is the whole point of an introduction. "I'd like to introduce my friend Bill to you" came from a time when you didn't walk up to someone and introduce yourself. Back then it just wasn't done. To meet someone required a formal introduction, which carried an unspoken guarantee: "I know this person, and he or she is trustworthy." Listening to someone is a way of quickly building a connection that reassures the other person you are of good character. This connection is a great benefit of skillful listening.

When you listen, you're liked. When you listen, you *show* respect and, in turn, you *get* respect. Want to be the life of a party? Want to make a good impression at your next professional meeting? Be quiet but be an active listener. Make it about the other person. Be a listener, and you will be the high point of the meeting. People will go away feeling a bond with you, because you used your skills to focus on them.

Listening creates connection, and to be successful in business and in life, we *need* connection. Listening well pays off in connections founded upon respect. When you listen to others, you will earn the right to be heard, and you will have their respect because you first showed them respect when you listened to them.

A second dividend that comes with listening and connection is you will have a greater influence on those with whom you are connected. Others are much more prone to allow us to influence them when we listen to them first, and skillful listening affords us the opportunity to impact and influence others.

GENERATIONS

Listening well provides you a roadmap to the different generations and the ability to relate to each of them.

There are four generations in the workplace right now, and while there are fewer of the World War II generation (or traditionalists) every day, there is a new generation following generation Y, or the millennial babies. Books, videos, and training seminars deal with this topic and how to understand each group. The method is to present the ways each of these generations regard work, leisure time, and their approach to life.

The only problem is while these principles are generally true, there are variations. For example, how about a "gen Y" that was born in Des Moines, who is the middle child of a Lutheran pastor? Does she think like the gen Y who is a first-born, Jewish, and has lived in Brooklyn all his life?

I am a baby boomer. I understand the "me" generation, but other generations confound me. I was pretty independent of my parents growing up. As an adult I tried not to depend on them or rely on them for emotional support. I assumed being independent as a young adult is universal and normal, at least for baby boomers, but my assumption was wrong.

My sons, a gen X-Y and a gen Y, have a different perspective. They like for me to be involved in their lives. They want to talk business, they want to visit, they come to me for advice, and they and their wives want to go out with us. That's just *different* for me.

When I was their age, I would have never wanted to hang out with my parents. When our children were young, we had teacher-parent conferences. Now, Gen Ys have "meet my boss" conferences where they introduce their parents to their supervisors. This is way over the top for a baby boomer!

The point is we *are* different. We all belong to cultures, and each of those has its own subcultures, and within those are even more subcultures. There is no way we can learn all those subtle differences in these many cultures. But deep, powerful listening allows us to pick up on the subtle nuances of every person's unique perspective.

Skillful listeners have the tools to comprehend the generational differences in cultures as well as *other* cultures and nationalities. They understand you can listen and relate to diverse points of view without embracing or agreeing with that point of view.

This mindset permits one to approach others with openness and curiosity. This allows the person from a generation or culture to feel safe to disclose his or her customs and values. It is one of the great dividends of listening and allows us to quickly hone in on the speaker's preferences.

So while you cannot know everything there is to know about every generation, you can quickly build rapport and come to a basic understanding of the values of a person's generational strata by attending to his or her words and creating a map in your mind of his or her particular culture.

One of the benefits of listening is it closes the generation gap for those who are skilled practitioners at listening.

MANAGING CONFLICT

The intent listener will enjoy the benefits of being able to manage conflict much better. It is impossible for two human beings to spend much time together without having conflict.

As the bumper sticker reads, *Conflict Happens!* It's part of life, but the ability to listen well pays off big dividends in the realm of conflict.

Most conflicts are caused by misunderstanding, poorly communicated expectations, or by not communicating at all.

The powerful listener is able to draw out the real needs of the speaker with intentional listening. When people feel heard, conflict diminishes because skillful listening allows expectations to be safely and clearly expressed, and misunderstandings are minimized.

While there will always be conflict, those who listen well will manage it better, because he or she will slow the conversation down by not arriving at any premature conclusions during the perception and processing stages. Taking the time to reflect back the words the listener is hearing will disarm conflict.

CORPORATE BENEFITS

As a manager, powerful listening is a way of showing concern for your employees. It creates a connection that fosters commitment and trust. Skilled employees are promoted into management because they excelled at a particular skill or job. They mastered the required abilities and became managers to model those qualities to others. While the new boss has reached his or her new position because of work skills, it is his or her proficiency at people skills that will now be required to keep him or her there.

Managers wear the mediator hat from time to time and are required to deal with interpersonal conflict. Your ability to listen will enable you to create win-win solutions. Managers who listen well understand the generational context of their employees as well as their personal proclivities and what motivates them. Listening will provide the information you need to encourage them and to provide meaningful rewards.

A study of managers at a large hospital system revealed the ability of the manager to listen well accounted for 40 percent of the variance in leadership ability. People don't leave a job; they leave a manager or supervisor. And most of those who leave report their boss simply didn't listen to them.

The manager who places a priority on developing great listening skills is preparing for continued success. For a manager, the benefit of skilled listening is that it makes his or her job a lot more productive with a lot less conflict.

CORPORATE ALIGNMENT

When organizations build a culture that encourages listening, they benefit from corporate alignment. When everyone knows exactly where the company is headed, the operation is less prone to conflict, teamwork results, and the entire organization works better, which in turn causes a higher return on investment.

The CEO of a company has a vision for where he wants that company to go and how he wants to get it there. The success of that company rests on how well those following the leader share in that vision and are truly aligned behind that leader.

You know you're in trouble if you're the general and you're leading the charge, and you look over your shoulder only to see that half of your troops are headed in a different direction.

Alignment is essential for organizational success. Impaired alignment is costly. Communication mistakes add up to a tremendous cost for misalignment. A culture of listening is a powerful antidote for misalignment. Being able to listen powerfully and "play back" what you've heard either lets your CEO know you got the message correctly or you didn't.

When people are listening at every level, there is a higher degree of efficiency because you're not spending time and resources fixing what went awry.

Misalignment comes from a failure to listen, and it is a costly proposition. A company consultant recounts an incident where a manager requested some booklets to be published. There was a breakdown in listening in the chain of command, and they ended up with two thousand booklets on the wrong topic. This failure to listen was costly and could easily have been avoided. It is an example of a failure to communicate or, more precisely, a failure to listen.

Alignment reminds me of an old carpenter's saying: measure twice, cut once. Perhaps a new proverb might go *companies that listen twice as much only have to work half as hard.*

The benefits of skillful listening at the corporate level are alignment, increased productivity, and of course, a greater return on investment.

PROJECT MANAGEMENT

Those who are charged with the task of bringing together stakeholders, stockholders, and other interested parties must, at all times, prioritize skillful listening. Successful execution requires everyone to be on the same page. This can only be done with careful listening.

Skilled responses are essential, as the manager must ensure he or she is hearing and conceptualizing what the stakeholder wants. While at the outset, a project might be clearly defined, still much can happen, and the path to the finish line is often an unpredictable course.

Frequently, there are hidden, unexpected issues that come to light requiring conversations, feedback, and joint decisions. Skillful listeners effectively navigate these issues much better. It is impossible to manage a project where, because of misunderstandings, half of the stakeholders are pulling in one direction, and the other half in another.

For the project manager, the benefit of skillful listening is the ability to ensure everyone is on the same page throughout the lifespan of the project.

TEAMWORK

In the book *The Five Dysfunctions of a Team,* Patrick Leoncioni puts *lack of trust* and *fear of conflict* at the top of the team dysfunction list. Trust comes from knowing a person. Knowing comes when people listen to each other. Good listeners manage conflict better than others. The good listener understands the speaker needs to be heard and that being heard will do more to assuage anger and conflict than anything else. Good listeners are the backbone of good teams and teamwork.

YES, BUT...

When I train folks about the benefits of powerful listening, I often hear objections, especially from managers and executives.

"This listening and playing back what I hear makes for a long, drawn-out conversation and wastes a lot of time." Or, "When I stop to really listen and reflect back what I hear, it feels awkward, or worse, it sounds like I'm agreeing with the other person." The one I hear most often is "I don't want to be a therapist or a confidante for my employees. I am not their mother."

All of these lines of thinking miss the point: you can't afford *not* to listen. *Not* listening *is* the waste of time, *not* listening and missing the point sets the stage for really awkward moments later on, and *not* listening to your employees leaves them anxious and uncertain of whether or not expectations are clear for both of you. This breeds disengagement, which is toxic in the workplace.

Remember, people don't leave a job, they leave a supervisor, and the cost of replacing an employee is high. The clearest benefit of a culture of listening in the workplace is a stable workforce. The benefits of listening in the workplace are well worth the time. You can't afford not to listen.

ON A PERSONAL LEVEL

As you become a great listener, the big payoff comes in richer, more satisfying relationships with the people in your personal circle of friends as well as acquaintances.

As you become more "present" and focused on what they have to say, they will treat you better. They will feel respected, and they will respect you more. You will find yourself spending a lot less time in conflict with others, and people will seek your friendship because you take the time to listen to them.

Learning to listen actively, reflectively, and empathically is great for business, but there is an even deeper benefit that surpasses business and everyday life. The benefit of ARE listening is it opens the door to deeper, more satisfying relationships with the people you love.

In the movie *Shadowlands*, about the life of author C.S. Lewis, a student confides in Lewis that the student's father told him, "We read to discover we are not alone." I think the same holds true for listening.

We listen to discover we are not alone. When we listen to others, we soften the cosmic isolation we, and those around us, instinctively feel. Listening links us to each other and to humanity. We discover we have much more in common than what separates us, and we are reassured we are not alone.

Listening to others allows you to enjoy people and makes for deeper, more satisfying relationships. Listening is the most powerful aphrodisiac for lovers. When men begin to listen to their wives, sexual intimacy is enhanced. Deep, intimate listening—where there are no barriers—is a metaphor for na-kedness, and in order to be sexual, most people must take off their clothes. Deep listening is emotional disrobing. The ben-efits are obvious.

Whether in the boardroom or in the bedroom, powerful listening improves your quality of life, which is the best benefit of all. Learning powerful listening is an act of self-denial. But the one who benefits the most is you. You will find success and rich relationships to be some of many dividends you will enjoy as a result of making the commitment to becoming a better listener.

ACTIVITIES: CONSIDER THE BENEFITS OF LISTENING FOR YOU

1. Think about your personal life. Make a list of all the benefits that come from using ARE listening as you focus on others around you.

2. Think about your work life. Make a list of all the benefits that come from using ARE listening as you focus on others around you.

3. If you were a salesman, how would you "sell" the benefits of skillful ARE listening?

Chapter Twelve

A LIFELONG QUEST

"I have no special talents.
I am only passionately curious."
Albert Einstein

Getting older means eventually you have this great realization the clock of life is ticking, and you're not going to live forever. Often, that realization becomes the incentive to get more serious about taking care of your health.

My wife and I hit that stage a few years ago and decided to take action, so we went shopping for a treadmill. We found a rather pricey model at a well-known department store. With all its whistles and bells, this particular machine promised to make the ordeal of walking in place less boring, if that's even possible.

Since it seemed like a worthwhile investment, we bought it, loaded it up in our van, and went straight home to get to work on our new healthy lifestyle.

We jumped in to an exercise regimen and remained faithful for about a year, until one day the thing just suddenly quit working.

Considering the price I paid for it, I expected that treadmill to last a lifetime. We called the store where we bought it, and they offered to send a repairman out to see what was wrong and provide a repair estimate. They were careful to let me know up front the estimate would cost me $99 and, if upon providing a diagnosis, I would allow them to fix the machine at the same time, they would apply the cost of the estimate to the repair bill.

We scheduled the repair. The technician arrived on the appointed date and time and took a few minutes to determine the treadmill motor was toast. He offered to repair it for about $500. If I would allow him to fix it while he was there, he would waive the cost of the estimate and only charge us for the repair. However, that offer was only good if I had him fix it right then and there.

I don't like to make financial decisions on the spur of the moment, and I also have this stubborn streak. So when I feel like I'm being pushed into something against my own will, I balk. True to form, I planted my feet, wrote him a check for the estimate, and sent him on his way.

Later that day, I got curious about the cost of the repair, so I "googled" my treadmill model and found I could get an exact replacement motor for about a hundred bucks. I asked myself, "How hard can it be to replace a treadmill motor?" After having assured myself that it can't be that big a deal, I ordered it.

When the motor arrived, I recruited one of my sons to help me switch it out. As we opened up the covering and prepared to change motors, he paused and told me we ought to just try cleaning the brushes on the motor before we went to all that trouble. We unscrewed two little plastic ports on either side of the motor, removed the brushes, cleaned them, put them back in, and turned the motor on. And it worked!

At first I was elated. And then, as the reality of the situation set in, I got angry with the technician for taking my money and not telling me the truth about my machine. The more I thought about what happened, the angrier I felt. I was steamed the rest of that day, and the next day, I was *still* steamed.

The following day, I called the store and told them I needed to speak to someone about a complaint. The customer service person who came on the line sounded like she was young and unsullied by the trials of life. In her perky little sunshine voice, she asked me what the problem was. I let go with both barrels. I told her in no uncertain terms just how angry I was because their technician took my money and misdiagnosed a simple problem.

Then she did the unexpected. Instead of getting defensive or escalating the conflict, she remained calm and even seemed to take my side by commenting I was really angry about this and she didn't blame me at all for feeling that way. She just started to listen to me and reflect back my feelings.

She was attentive, kind, and had the patience of Job. She never got defensive. Every time I would complain or gripe about something else, she would calmly repeat my words back to me and validate my feelings. Over the next couple of minutes, I began to calm down. At first, I was just aware my anger was dissipating, but, as the fog in my mind lifted, it dawned on me: I was being listened to *by an expert!* As a therapist, I knew *exactly* what she was doing. But it felt so good, I just went along with her and let her do it anyway.

At the end of the conversation, I didn't get my money back. I don't even remember whether or not I got an apology, but it was sure wonderful to be heard! I felt a lot better due to nothing more than a sympathetic soul who was willing to hear me out—all because someone knew the importance of listening and how to do it well.

When I present training seminars, I always use this illustration because it is a powerful reminder of the importance of listening for all walks of life. I was well practiced in reflective listening, and I knew exactly what the customer representative was doing. When it came to a choice of letting her know I was *on* to her or just going along with her, I chose to go along.

Even knowing what was up, I craved being understood, being heard, and being valued. That, to me, underscores the importance of this concept. Listening is powerful! It had the power to move me from anger to acceptance, with little apparent effort on the part of the person at the other end of the phone line.

So if by now you are convinced of the importance of listening and realize that you need to get with the program, where do you start? Just like a good exercise program, you make a commitment to your goal and stick with it.

GETTING THERE

If your listening skills are deficient, how do you go from where you are right now to where you want to be? The answer is the same way you get to Carnegie Hall: *practice, practice, practice!* So how do you remember to practice? Hopefully over the last eleven chapters, you've come to understand the importance of listening in every area where we interact with others.

Becoming a great listener begins with seeing the problem, understanding how vital listening is in the workplace (or anyplace), and understanding the need for improvement. Before you can make communication better, you must recognize there actually is a problem.

The second step is making active, reflective, empathic (ARE) listening a priority by charting the course and continuing to aim for that goal. Remain committed to continually sharpening your skills and your awareness level of those around you.

I wish I could tell you you'll eventually master the art of powerful listening, but I can't. The bad news is we never get there. We *never* perfect the art of listening. We're human. We get tired, emotional, weak. These impair our ability to be the perfect listener.

Throughout the span of their careers, doctors practice medicine and attorneys practice law. I don't worry about my doctor "practicing" medicine, because I am confident he is already good, and practice is his method of always improving his skills. In the same way we practice, our striving to be better should *always* be the priority.

Becoming a great listener involves trying and failing and trying and failing again. You'll do great some days, and you'll feel like a rank amateur on others.

Remember you are moving toward a goal you'll never be perfect at in this life. Nevertheless, aiming at nothing will get you there every time. So to get where you're going, you consistently strive for continuous improvement. There is *always* something you can *always* do a little better next time.

What I can promise is you will get better and you will find people will respond to you with warmth and respect if you understand what is required and practice the steps required for skillful listening.

Begin to listen more and speak less, and learn to treasure the uniqueness of every human being. You will find a joy and satisfaction in powerful listening. You'll also feel more confident about yourself, because you will remember details about people, and feel connected to them in a positive way that impacts both of you. Your life will be richer as you delve into the tapestry of other people's lives.

The greatest step toward becoming a great listener is just having the desire and commitment to accomplish this.

For a moment, let your imagination run wild, and picture this scenario: the president of the United States just signed into law a bill requiring every citizen in the United States must learn to play the piano. After the revolt is over, you would have to get on with the task at hand. You would need to buy a piano and find a time and place to practice, get a teacher, buy some music, budget time and money for lessons, and then invest the time to practice your skills. Now that's a sizeable commitment.

Having that scenario in your mind, consider this: your boss tells you that in order to keep your job, you must become an expert listener. You wouldn't need to buy anything—no piano to move, no teacher, no books. You wouldn't have to schedule practice time, because the world would be your practice room, and every encounter would be an opportunity to hone those skills.

In order to become a great listener, you must make the commitment to listening well *all* the time, and then you must also practice your skills as consistently as you can.

To do this, you make the quest to become a great listener part of your values and life mission statement. Then you look at every encounter with another person as a golden opportunity to practice your skills. Make a lifetime commitment to becoming a better listener, and that is exactly what you will become.

Consider every interaction with another human being as an opportunity to practice your skills, and the whole world becomes your practice room!

In chapter two, we discussed the importance of listening to your children. Listening starts before the child is born, and as infants children listen to their mothers and learn to regulate their own emotions through that interaction. We also discussed how a parent who listens and responds appropriately to that child instills a sense of security, enabling the child to make healthy transitions through the different developmental stages and into adulthood. The time and effort spent attending to your child, carrying on conversations, and perceiving, processing, and responding to him or her also provides a model for his or her behavior as adults.

So the child benefits from healthy development and is equipped to listen to others. Children become well-adjusted because they were listened to and, in turn, grow up with great listening skills and are equipped to be successful in life.

TORNADO REVISITED

The devastation of an Oklahoma twister brings to us back around to one simple point: You can make an impact on the world by just listening.

The boxcar sitting in the middle of the field after the tornado reminded me of Dorothy's house after it landed somewhere over the rainbow. There was something so surreal about a massive mound of steel sitting so far from the railroad tracks and from any road. It was as if someone had just plucked a toy train car off its tracks and gently placed it in a meadow. It was plain to see. My eyes said it was there, but my brain wasn't able to comprehend the picture. It just didn't make sense.

Every time I drove past it, I wondered where it came from. How high did it get lifted? How was it able to land without getting damaged? I also wondered how they were going to get it out of there.

The boxcar in the field left me at once intrigued and disturbed. It was a reminder of how big a rift was torn in the fabric of a community after the tornadoes ravaged Oklahoma. After that fateful day, nothing made sense. As with the boxcar in the field, the effects were plain to see, but still they were so incomprehensible. They completely overwhelmed one's capacity to comprehend.

The boxcar scene reminded me of the many lives upended and the folks who wondered if life would ever be normal again.

The task of an entire community working to heal from the psychic damage inflicted by the storms seemed staggering. The stories therapists heard were heartbreaking. It was difficult to even imagine this community getting back to normal for a long, long time.

Yet, little by little, the community did recover.

The tornadoes of 1999 changed Oklahoma forever. In time, however, the community did rebuild.

Eventually homes were built where the rubble of destroyed houses once stood. Folks found and identified lost treasures strewn across the state. Strangers returned pictures and priceless memories from distant counties. Families began to put the pieces of their shattered lives back together. People worked through the pain and trauma of this terrible event, and eventually life did return to normal.

We were all changed.

Every year, tornado season comes around once again. Oklahomans are more careful to listen to the weather forecast, and this time around they take severe storm warnings much more seriously.

The community also continued the internal healing process. Children quit having nightmares, test scores for students returned to normal, problems with concentration and conflict at school and home diminished, and people worked through their fears.

As for the therapists, they continued to provide counseling to victims for years after the event.

The federal government frequently brought in subject-matter experts to train the front-line caregivers in order to make available the very best care for the victims.

Once a month or so, an expert would spend a day or two with us, and we enjoyed training by world-renowned psychologists on the effects of trauma and post-traumatic stress disorder. We heard the cutting-edge research from the best and brightest in the field of traumatology. The federal government invested hundreds of thousands of dollars to make available the most up-to-the-moment information so that we could provide effective health care to these victims.

The great irony is all of this can be reduced to one simple thought: if you simply listen to people, *really listen to them,* by being fully present as they tell their story, they will find their own path to health and success, and they will get better on their own. And that's exactly what happened.

We listened.

They got better.

That *is* the incredible power of listening.

ACTIVITIES: THIRTY DAYS TO GREAT LISTENING

1. For the next thirty days, plan a specific time each day when you will do your best to use all your listening skills to listen patiently with your body, with your voice, and with your mind.

2. For the next thirty days, schedule a thirty-minute period where you can just sit and be quiet. During this time, clear your mind and listen for God to speak to you.

3. For the next thirty days, make a point to use your very best listening skills every time you must attend a meeting, a party, or any function where there are a lot of people. Be quiet, be present, and be active as a listener.

4. For the next thirty days, rehearse skillful listening in your mind. Anytime you have a one-on-one meeting with an employee or coffee with a friend or associate, before the encounter visualize yourself being totally caught up in the other's story. Rehearse in your mind how you will actively listen, reflect well, and empathize with the other person.

ABOUT THE AUTHOR

Tim Hast is an acclaimed speaker, consultant and business and life coach. His many years in the counseling field and previously as the owner of a service-based company lend an experiential and research-based authority to his energetic, engaging, and information-packed workshops.

His coaching and group presentations are guided by two beliefs. First, that people have more potential than they realize; unleashing that potential is his passion. Second, that our ability to manage interpersonal relationships is directly connected to success in business and in life. While excellent technical skills will get a person hired, the ability to relate to others is what moves us to the top.

Tim provides keynotes, seminars and coaching on interpersonal skills in the workplace. His topics include:

- Listening
- Communication
- Conflict resolution
- Understanding and managing emotions
- Teambuilding and team leadership
- The psychology of effective leadership
- Understanding personality types
- Dealing with angry customers/coworkers
- Everything you need to know about managing people

He is an Everything DiSC® Authorized Partner, providing DiSC® personality assessments and 363 evaluations in diverse settings. He specializes in group training on how to understand and work efficiently with others.

Tim lives in Edmond, Oklahoma with his wife Ruthie, a Licensed Professional Counselor. They work together in their business, Encore Life Skills.

Contact Tim:

coach@att.net

www.encorelifeskills.com

Find him on Linkedin

CPSIA information can be obtained at www.ICGtesting.com
Printed in the USA
LVOW06s2059130815

450011LV00033B/1149/P